TEACHERS OF THE WORLD, UNITE!

Sebastian de Assis

To Barb,
Whose interest in education for
human development can make
a difference to the future of
humanity.

The Educational Center Press

First Edition

ISBN 0-9700722-0-1
Library of Congress Control Number: 00-133080

Published by The Educational Center Press
P.O. Box 443
Corvallis, OR 97339-0443

Book Cover Design: Matt Dahm
Typesetting: Tamera Mosher

Printed in the United States of America

Dedication

This book is dedicated to the living spirit of Socrates, the martyr of education for freedom, and all of his noble successors; particularly, Jean Jacques Rousseau, Johann Pestalozzi, Rudolf Steiner, A.S. Neill, Paulo Freire, and to all educators who toil for the cause of human development in freedom.

Acknowledgement

I want to acknowledge the unswerving support and encouragement of my best friend and wife Tiera de Assis. She is the one who challenged me to write this manuscript.

TABLE OF CONTENTS

THE TEACHER

Let me see if I have this right. You want me to go into that room with all those kids and fill their every waking moment with a love for learning. Not only that, but I am also to instill a sense of pride in their ethnicity, modify disruptive behavior and observe them for signs of abuse. I am to fight the war on drugs and sexually transmitted diseases, check their backpacks for guns and knives, and raise their self-esteem. I am to teach them patriotism, good citizenship, sportsmanship and fair play; how to balance a checkbook; and how to apply for a job. I am to check their head for lice, maintain a safe environment, recognize signs of potential antisocial behavior, offer advice, write letters of recommendation for student employment and scholarships, encourage respect for the cultural diversity of others, and, oh yes, teach, always making sure I give the girls in my class 50 percent of my attention. I am required by my contract to work on my own time (summers and evenings) and at my own expense toward additional certification and master's degree, to sponsor the cheerleaders, or the sophomore class (my choice). After school, I am to attend committee and faculty meetings and participate in staff development training to maintain my current certification and employment status. I am to be a paragon of virtue, such that my very presence will awe my students into being obedient and respectful of authority. I am to do all of this with just a piece of chalk, a bulletin board and a few books (some of which I may have to purchase myself). For doing this, I am to be paid a starting salary that, in some states, qualifies my family for food stamps. Is that all?

Anonymous

INTRODUCTION

A new revolution is emerging in the twenty-first century. Unlike the revolutions of the past two centuries, the new revolution is not of political, economic or social nature--though it will certainly affect all of these areas. It is a revolution in education. At the core of this revolutionary movement lies a professional class that has long been responsible for the development of the individual outside the family unit: We, the teachers of the world.

From pre-school to graduate school, students, parents, society and civilization itself have bestowed upon us the enormous responsibility of preparing children and young adults to become independent, self-sustaining and productive individuals. Unfortunately, we have been failing our honorable duty; not because of low standardized test results and poor academic performance, as we are often blamed and criticized for, but for basically preparing students to fulfill economic functions while neglecting their complex developmental needs.

In reality, we have been unwittingly manipulated by economic and political forces that control the educational system. These forces proclaim that the educational crisis is exclusively related to the inadequacy of schooling and the incompetence of teaching professionals. They are reluctant to admit that the crisis in education is nothing but a reflection of a broad and complex social debacle. Truthfully, the crisis is ignited by an obsession with economic expansion motivated by selfishness, greed and unbridled competition in the pursuit of profit.

Hence, the appalling violence in our school yards, the high incidence of teen-pregnancy, drug and alcohol abuse, among other equally serious ills in our schools (society), are manifestations of a social ethos in which violence, sex, alcohol and drugs (legal and illegal) are valuable commodities glamorized in the media and entertainment business. Nevertheless, the educational system in general, and teachers in particular, become the scapegoats of this social tragedy.

Indeed, the challenges are daunting and countless. Consequently, the role of the teacher in the development of the human being (each individual member of society) becomes even more accentuated. Are we going to continue to be mere cogs in the immense economic-political machinery, diligently training the labor force for the job-market, or are we going to take action in the transformation of the educational system into a more humanizing learning process based on freedom and human development? Are we going to continue to focus our attention primarily on the training of the worker-to-be, or are we going to dedicate ourselves to the complex developmental needs of the individual human? And who is to determine what the priorities of education must be?

The only way to find answers is by asking questions. Thus, using a simplified Socratic approach as a guiding light, this book raises some fundamental questions on the nature, function, purpose of education and the teaching class. It aims to encourage every teacher to raise his own questions in the pursuit of fundamental truths. The answers themselves could ignite an education revolution in which the individual human, not the individual worker, becomes the powerful hub of the educational wheel.

Another important objective of this book is to help teachers to become fully aware of their tremendous responsibilities, duties, identity, value, and the power of the profession in the social, economic and political arena. It is also aimed at inspiring solidarity among the members of the only profession that is ubiquitously present in all professions.

While the gap between the highly sophisticated intellectual individual and the emotionally and spiritually underdeveloped human being widens, the time has come for the teaching class to stand up and speak out for a positive transformation of the educational system--and the society it serves. Let the twenty-first century be the harbinger of a new era in reform of education. Let humanity prevail over the oppressing automatization of the human spirit. Let our responsibility to human development be the only dictating factor in our profession.

The time has come in which we must make crucial decisions. We have reached the turning point that will determine the destiny of the human species and the future of civilization; and the gravity of the challenges we face demand immediate action. Hence, together, in unison, we cry out: Teachers of the world, unite!

NOTE:
1. The word "spiritual" which often appears in the text is devoid of any religious context per se. Instead, it refers to that intrinsic component of humanity, which has been smothered by the technological-materialistic emphasis of modern industrial societies.

2. The word Humanities has been purposefully capitalized throughout the text in order to emphasize the importance of the disciplines in education for human development.

PART I

THE TEACHING CLASS

What does it mean to be a teacher?

The teaching profession is a relatively modern occupation. It was not until the mid-1820's in Europe that candidates for teaching positions had to abide by certain pedagogical requirements of the newly established profession. In the United States, teacher preparation did not gain acceptance until the 1830's, when economic development brought about by industrialization, stimulated the expansion of public education under the influence of Horace Mann (1796-1859); "the father of American public education."

Before the 1800's, education was provided by private tutors; and, if we go further back in history to ancient Greece, by slaves. These untrained and uncertified teachers were mostly studious individuals whose thirst for knowledge made them a coveted commodity for the dominant classes (either as a property or a servant), since education was considered a luxury of few. This subservient characteristic of the teaching class still prevails in a very subtle way in the core of society; and it is clearly revealed in the value attributed to teachers, both in professional status and remuneration.

Today, teachers go through a comprehensive preparation program leading to certification that encompasses three specific components: general education, specialization and professional education development. The many college graduates who have not gone through this "training" process, unlike the coveted independent scholars of the past, are not allowed to teach in public schools; many of whom are extremely talented and loving professionals. They are denied the opportunity to serve their community with their genuine calling to teach. The problem lies in the fact that education has changed from a craft that spurs curiosity and a love of learning (the art of teaching) to a quasi-technical trade. The purpose of the latter is to train students how to read, write and learn math skills (literacy and numeracy), in a process which the art of education is subdued to the demands of economic functionalism.

However, a teacher, a genuine educator, is much more than a rigorously trained professional who merely instructs and conveys information to an apathetic audience of uninterested learners. The authentic teacher is a professional with an ontological vocation to enrich the individual lives of students, while contributing to the prosperity of all. He is an active social transformational agent who never forsakes the principles of her responsibility. His loyalty and educational objectives are intrinsically related to individual human development, and he does not betray this commitment nor does he surrender his power to any external force that does not support his professional purpose. She is caring and loving, and the quality and integrity of her character teaches just as much as her knowledge of subject matters. She holds high professional ethics sustained by a solid foundation of love for helping others to grow and prosper.

Unfortunately, the current educational system controlled by powerful political and economic forces cannot embrace this vision, for the latter have specific objectives of their own. Often times their interest frontally clashes with the interest of integral human development; after all, what corporations, or career politicians associated with them, would be interested in an educational system that promotes critical thinking? Such initiative would certainly impede the easy manipulation of ideas by the corporate owned mass-media. Furthermore, teaching children, from a very young age, that they should care for others in a spirit of solidarity and cooperation could ruin the unfettered competitive doctrine that rules the dominant economic system, where neither solidarity nor cooperation is welcome.

Nevertheless, the cry for education reform comes from the same circles that aggravate the problem; at least from the stand point of the developmental needs of the individual human. They want better standardized test results, better math skills, better technology, better trained teachers, better schools. They just do not seem to be equally concerned with the comprehensive human development of John and Mary; instead, they are obsessively preoccupied with the training of the generalist and specialized worker. And when this objective is not properly achieved according to specific requirements, they point the finger at teachers who are one of the most dedicated, hard-working and undervalued corps of professionals.

Although education has changed dramatically in the last century, the teaching class has not followed suit. However, the circumstances and challenges we face in the twenty-first century demand that teachers reevaluate their role, function and political power--and take action for change! As the economic system depends on education to produce a literate workforce, humanity has entrusted teachers to serve the integral needs of human development according to three specific categories: Mind (intellect), Heart (emotions) and Spirit (soul)--the physical body is also included, but as a vehicle that allows the entire process to unravel. So, which interests should teachers serve? For the conscientious educator the answer is self-evident.

Why do you teach?

According to a survey conducted by the National Education Association in the 1990's, 66% of teachers began their career motivated by a desire to work with young people, while 37% referred to the significance of education in society. However, in contrast with the NEA survey, the Department of Education released a report stating that 22% of teachers quit within three years, while in inner city schools 50% abandon the profession within the same period of time. Matching the two conflicting data, the inference is obvious: idealism can be brutally tampered by the daily realities of the profession.

Because of the astounding shortage of teachers in the United States, many young people are choosing a career in education as a sure way to employment. The demand is transforming education into an easy pathway to a professional career. Those are the individuals who will endorse with their names the national statistics on teachers' drop out rates. As soon as they realize the bureaucratic web they are caught in, the long hours and work done at home, the stressful field trips, fretting about students joining gangs, parents' complaints, criticism from school officials, among a barrage of other problems, then, they realize the "easy job" with summers off was not the dream situation after all. They quit.

However, there are a great number of teachers (the 66% of the statistics mentioned above) whose calling to education was so irrepressibly strong that they could not resist it. They are the ones who make an extraordinary impact on a child's life; whose contribution helps society become a better community for all. Unfortunately, they, too, fall victim to the drop out paradigm that prevails in the teaching profession nowadays. Thus, knowing the reasons, difficulties and rewards of being a teacher is imperative in the struggle to sustaining the commitment.

For those who will beat the odds and retire after a long successful teaching career, three elements with one common denominator are likely to be present: a love of teaching, a love of learning and a love of children. Like chemical elements, they blend in and produce a reaction that translates into a passion for education, which students notice and respond to. If you teach because you love it (teaching, learning and children), then, the personal factor of your professional quandary has been resolved. You know your own personal reasons to be a teacher. The next step is to question why do you teach in terms of your social function.

In addition to a love of teaching, learning and children, genuine teachers also have a strong desire to make a contribution in a much larger scale. Assisting in the individual development of students is the source of personal gratification that rewards a career objective. But a teacher's sense of accomplishment is incomplete if she does not actively participate in the sociological and historical changes of her time. Even though this participation may seem minimum and insignificant, the enormous social responsibility intrinsic to the teaching profession requires the teacher to become involved in social issues. Here again, the teacher must know why he teaches.

At first she may be confounded and overwhelmed with the task at hand. After all, what is a teacher to do in a classroom in some obscure small town that can make a difference for positive social transformation? Interestingly, this predicament is tantamount to our own democratic process. The citizen who does not believe his vote can impact the results of general elections will remain apathetic--and apolitical--to the decision-making process of the nation. Similarly, the teacher who does not believe he can transform social reality through his work in the classroom is equally unconcerned. Like the absent voter who forfeits her democratic rights--and civil duty--the teacher who does not carry out her responsibility to educate his pupils on pressing social problems is guilty by omission. Thus, if you vote because you believe you can make a difference, do exactly the same in your classroom. If you don't do either, begin doing both-- immediately!

One final detail remains to be clarified: how can you bring awareness of complex and challenging social problems to young children? Easy: through the Humanities. Every child, as a human being, can understand the language of arts, music, drama, etc. By creating a comprehensive Humanities program emphasizing the social challenges of our times, the door is wide open for awareness to come in; and subsequently, action for positive change. However, a caveat must be inserted here: this entire process must occur in absolute freedom of learning, without any interference from the teacher's own belief system. Proselytizing has no room in the education of a free society.

Knowing the reasons you chose to teach can make an extraordinary difference in your life as a teacher; not to mention the student and society you serve. It should be a prerequisite for any teaching candidate in this country. Unfortunately, the demand for commodity labor in our factory schools only requires well-trained--and certified-- technicians of information, not educators of quality devoted to human development.

What is the educational role of the teacher?

At the core of the educational system the teacher is, and always will be, the most important element. Her gargantuan professional responsibility is tantamount to the responsibility of a surgeon whose patient's life depends on his medical knowledge and his skills wielding operating tools. The difference, however, is that the teacher's responsibility has a lifetime impact on the development of a human being. Parents entrust their sons and daughters to the members of this noble profession, hoping their children will be cared for and their needs properly met. Regrettably, because of the misconception of what education is supposed to be, parents, in general, view the academic benefit as the primary concern regarding their children's education. After all, their beloved children will need to have a good job in order to be financially successful--the most significant social value we erroneously embrace. What parents ignore is that children will also need to have a good life, and that involves several other aspects of which professional accomplishment and financial stability are just two elements in a complex web of achievements.

Indeed, the role of the teacher has always been of enormous importance to the success of the educational system. Aware of this fact, the bureaucrats of education, their cohorts in the economic-political machinery, the misinformed public and misled parents are promptly ready to blame members of the teaching class for the misfortunes and failures in our schools. Although there are bad apples in any professional tree, teachers are particularly singled out for the deficiencies and flaws of education; namely, poor academic performance and low standardized test results. Rarely, if ever, do the "experts" of educational policy note that the social and individual circumstances of our time have changed more rapidly than technological development itself; and this is not, by any means, an overstatement. In the 1940's, for instance, common daily school problems were talking, chewing gum, making noise, running in the halls, getting out of line, wearing improper clothing, not putting paper in the wastebaskets among other misdemeanors. Today, our schools are plagued by drug and alcohol abuse, pregnancy, suicide, rape, robbery, assault, and, the most notorious of them all, mass-murder on school grounds. And remember: this is what teachers are dealing with on a regular basis.

In addition to the overwhelming emotional baggage that is dumped on teachers' laps every day, teachers in the inner city public schools also have special extra problems, ranging from children's malnutrition to mental, emotional and physical abuse. Meanwhile, nobody seems to address the issue of poverty as an outcome of economic expansion, escalating violence as a cultural trend, dysfunctional families who cannot make financial ends meet, youth hopelessness and their preoccupation with a future marred by a plethora of ecological, social and political problems as the main culprits to the educational crisis. Nevertheless, if the teacher cannot teach a child affected by some or all of these circumstances, he is to blame for failure. Occasionally, the focus of criticism is diverted to "uncaring parents" who do not take the time to study with their children. Never mind that time has become a luxury that parents who run the rat-race do not always have.

The truth is we are all responsible for the education of changing generations. Teachers, parents, government, business and society as a whole must share the load, because education involves and affects every individual and every aspect of social life. However, the role of the teacher in the educational process of a child is a particularly distinct one compared with that of everyone else. His work is categorized in three specific levels.

During the first years of schooling (kindergarten through fifth grade), the child is at an extremely vulnerable stage that requires special care and dedicated attention from the teacher. Rudolf Steiner (1861-1925), the founder of Waldorf Schools, considers the first seven years of a child's life as the imitative stage, when the child literally emulates her role models. This is the time when parents, teachers and the educational system of a society will greatly contribute--or be detrimental--to determining the type of person and learner the child will become. Consequently, if at this level the child is denied his inalienable right to a completely fulfilling childhood; that is, a childhood characterized by innocence and imagination and devoid of intellectual and social pressures, she will likely disclose the effects of a faulty foundation in adolescence, when academic, peer and other pressures are highly accentuated.

Since the child spends a considerable amount of time under the teacher's care, it is absolutely imperative for the teacher at the elementary level of education to be a nurturing and loving individual whose primary concern is to guide the child's natural process of self-discovery. This will pave the way to the later years of learning when intellectual, emotional and spiritual development will take place through studies and experiential learning.

Hence, the role of the elementary school teacher is that of a guardian angel of childhood; caring, loving, nurturing and protecting the child during the most important and beautiful time in human life: childhood. Furthermore, the elementary school teacher, as well as his colleagues in middle and high-school, must be well-acquainted with the Declaration of the Rights of the Child, adopted by the General Assembly of the United Nations on November 20, 1959--and make sure to enforce it as a professional duty.

At the elementary level, the role of the teacher is crucial. She has to be an instructor, a surrogate parent, a guide, a role model, and, ultimately, a trustworthy friend of the developing human being. As Gabriela Mistral (1889-1957), the Chilean poet and educator who was awarded the Nobel Prize for Literature in 1945 stated, "if you do not have a genuine love for children and a burning desire to help them grow, teaching is not a profession for you."

The middle-school years are the most challenging for both teachers and children. This is a difficult transitional phase in which the child crosses the tenuous bridge linking childhood to puberty. At this time, several biological, physiological, psychological and sociological changes begin to take place with the potential to wreak havoc in the maturing young person's life.

If the natural pressures of sheer existence were not enough, the educational system comes down on the pre-adolescent with excessive academic demands and strict rules of social conformity. Moreover, the economic functionalism of education becomes exacerbated as the pressure to produce, achieve and $ucceed assumes top priority. This is the time when liking or disliking school can generate perennial consequences. Hence, freedom of learning; that is, allowing and encouraging the student to excel in her natural talents and inclinations, be it writing poetry or studying quantum physics, can determine whether long-term learning will be successful or not.

In order to create an auspicious educational program at the middle-school level, innovative curricula and teacher's creativity in the art of teaching must be harmonious with freedom of learning. Such ingenuity in education should not be entirely bound to academic matters only; after all, there is much more to education than acquisition of information.

In addition to educational services of academic and social nature, the middle-school teacher plays a fundamental role in the development of character in the insecure pre-adolescent. Counseling skills are indispensable tools in guiding the middle-schooler toward a sound and safe adolescence that will lead to the development of a well-rooted person. Listening, regardless of how absurd the content may be, is imperative to successfully winning the confidence of the youngster under the teacher's care. Gratuitous criticism is a suicidal approach that defeats all efforts and purposes. Motivation and encouragement are infinitely more effective and helpful for the youngster striving to reach her utmost potential.

The modern high school has become a training program rather than an educational system. While we have been focusing on the technical and vocational approaches to learning, the quality of America's high schools has been declining continuously. The statistics backing up the facts are nothing short of appalling: 22% of our children live in poverty; crime among juveniles has increased 600% since the 1960's; the incidence of drug and alcohol abuse among children is dangerously high; America leads the world in teenage suicides; more teenagers become pregnant out of wedlock in the United States than in any other country. The statistics convey two clear messages: first, we are breeding a self-destructive generation that could seriously jeopardize individual and social development. The other message is even more obvious: the aggressive economic oriented educational system is failing miserably.

Therefore the conscientious high school teacher, in spite of the bureaucratic rules that limit his range of action, must promote critical thinking while addressing issues that are beyond the mundane acquisition of information. He should assist students to realize that without a sustainable environment and the elimination of poverty, intolerance, prejudice and so many other social maladies, they might not have a worthy existence at all; even if they succeed in their chosen professional career. The greatest good must be for the greatest number, if we are going to transform social chaos into harmonious living.

Unfortunately, at the high school level the potential role and influence of the teacher have been considerably diminished compared with the earlier years of schooling. Inferentially, it is at the elementary and middle school level that the role of the teacher is most crucial.

As influence on students wanes, the risks of teaching a group of hostile youngsters, especially in inner cities and poverty stricken areas, can range from assault to murder. Needless to say, the teaching profession is becoming an increasingly dangerous activity. Moreover, teachers should bear in mind that the dangers of teaching are not only related to the individual professionals in the classroom. Most importantly, teaching can also be a very dangerous activity when teachers unite and advocate an educational system based on freedom and human development, for the powerful dominating forces will likely become reactionary.

What is the political role of the teacher?

In theory, the teaching class should be one of the most powerful political forces in any nation. In reality, teachers exert minimum, if any, political influence in society outside organized unions.   -

Considering the ubiquitous character of this profession--every one in every field of work has been under the guidance and influence of teachers--the intrinsic, and yet ignored, political power associated with teaching professionals is phenomenal. Nevertheless, it is neither sufficiently exercised by individual teachers nor by the teaching class as a political voice. In fact, teachers' power has been relegated to organized labor unions and other small and inconspicuous organizations that struggle against bureaucratic forces and their archaic educational policies. Thus, a professional class that should exert unmatched political power in society, has become the pawn of other manipulative social forces. The time has come for teachers to reclaim the power the nature of the profession bestows upon them.

In the meantime, career politicians and other private interest groups have been cashing-in on the national obsession and negative propaganda of the educational crisis. While they reap the rewards by dictating how education should be run, the crisis remains fundamentally social in nature, and merely reverberates its negative echoes in the schools. These demagogues running for public office literally use the teaching class to enhance their images before the naive, misinformed and manipulated electorate. They purport to be resolutely committed to improving school accountability and teacher preparation, while promising that every child will learn to read by the end of third grade; a promise, like countless others they make, completely beyond the reach of their political role.

Eventually, their promises fail. And yet, they remain immune from public persecution, for they are quick to blame the fiasco on incompetent teachers and school officials. The latter professionals will be encouraged to find another line of work if the situation--improved academic performance "documented" by higher standardized test results--does not show improvement before reelection season. Not once do politicians allude the problem to poor budget management or inadequate funding of the educational system. They set high expectations for everyone but themselves.

In addition to usurping teachers' political and professional power, the coalition of politicians, bureaucrats and economic interests--supported by a misled public opinion--have been setting up various policies and rules that further enfeebles the teaching class. Mandatory performance exams for teachers to measure their knowledge in the subject matter they teach (the standardized test version for teachers), laws eliminating tenure for educators, pay raises linked to student performance, among other aggressive initiatives, are becoming a national trend; often times endorsed by teachers' unions. They want to improve education by weakening and demoralizing its main agent: the teacher. What an asinine strategy!

Although it is supposed to be the responsibility of schools of education to ensure that the teacher candidate is qualified to teach a particular discipline, these new policies of testing professionals who already are under enormous daily pressures are unacceptable. This additional pressure has not shown any signs of improvement in the educational crisis; on the contrary, it seems to have aggravated it, for more and more teachers are quitting the job and searching for new opportunities in other fields of work. There is a limit to abuse and unappreciation teachers are willing to take.

The argument buttressing these initiatives relates to what has been determined to be poor teacher performance; which indirectly becomes the answer to the problems of the educational crisis. Meanwhile, there is a parallel crisis that worsens simultaneously as strict rules, criticism, lack of appreciation and low salaries prevail: there is a seriously critical dearth of "commodity-teachers" to meet the growing demands of the education market.

According to the National Center for Education Statistics, 17.1% of new public school teachers abandon teaching within their first four years on the job; 9.3% of them leave after only a single year. There are other studies (like the ones mentioned earlier) that estimate the attrition rate at between 30% and 50% in the first five years, and 60% of teachers quit the profession altogether within ten years. These figures make new teachers the group most vulnerable to leaving their profession. Take these numbers and match them against the approximately two million new teachers that will be needed in the next ten years and we have a real educational crisis.

In the meantime, strict legislation and policies are regularly enacted, putting more pressure on the teaching profession. In the state of Oregon, for instance, a laundry-list size of instructions have come out recently. State lawmakers have decided that teachers must teach more about Oregon geography and civics, evaluate students' performance in physical education against state standards and focus on the Irish potato famine as part of the classroom curricula. Lawmakers also dictated that more class time must be spent on flag salutes and molding good character. They tried to push a little further with a proposal to urge students to wear uniforms, and require them to learn gun safety from the National Rifle Association, but the state governor vetoed them.

As a consequence of these measures, some superintendents in the state have complained that local power is being eroded, as the legislature is making teachers, principals and administrators feel uncomfortable. What used to be the responsibility of local school boards or the State Board of Education, is now in the hands of some retrograde career politicians.

But that is not all. Besides evaluating student and teacher performance through some inane standardized tests, the schools themselves are also being graded. This is causing a great deal of anxiety among teachers, principals and some superintendents who are worried their schools might not make the grade. Others even question the motivation of the legislature in requiring report cards in the first place. It certainly doesn't help the already hectic situation. Nevertheless, about forty states in the nation issue reports on individual schools, and a dozen of them give schools a rating, which is nothing other than collective performance evaluation of teachers.

All these measures and initiatives claiming to hold educators accountable for their job performance amount to an attack on the teaching class; a hard-working, undervalued and unappreciated corps of professionals. Weakening teachers' collective bargaining rights and driving down teachers' morale, only beget frustration and resentment among teachers. They already are overworked, burned out, underpaid--and fed up!

Meanwhile, the crackdown on the so-called subpar performance goes on. Using a system that links the evaluation of teachers' performance to those of students, without taking into consideration that students' progress involves numerous factors unrelated to school activities, is an unfair practice. Often times, students' performance is beyond the control of the classroom teacher.

Teachers have unjustifiably become the scapegoats of an educational crisis that is not responding to society's obsession with economic expansion. The crisis, however, does not lie in education per se, but in the terribly erroneous conception of education as a means to fulfill an economic function. At the red hot center of the crisis lies the emotionally underdeveloped and spiritually illiterate human being searching for the truth of an existence lost in the maddening pursuit of intellectual knowledge.

So, what are teachers to do? We must organize and take action--at once. Organize at the grassroots level; in every school, neighborhood, district, state, country--the world. Although unions are extremely important elements in this process, the power of individual awareness and direct participation of every one is of insurmountable value. We must also bear in mind that the opposite forces (bureaucrats, politicians, big business, the religious right, radical conservative groups, etc.), are currently dictating the rules of the game in a manner that they, not the teachers or the children whom we serve, will be victorious; unless, we decide to fight back. The honor of our profession demands it from us, and so do the children and the future, which belongs to them and to them only; a future that does not begin nor end with readiness to fulfill an economic function in a consumerist society gone berserk.

In reality, the political power of teachers is an untapped resource of social transformation that must be accessed. The crisis, not of the educational system but the immense challenges before us as we embark on a new millennium, requires the educator's commitment to her social responsibility in the classroom. That means, presenting the bare facts and the consequences of those facts in the historical process, so that evolving youngsters can make intelligent decisions about the future that belongs to them.

Thus, the political power of teachers lies in the professional commitment to foster the development of the human being for the sake of life itself, instead of producing labor-commodities for an economic system based on rapacious consumption that is the origin of the crisis itself.

Do teachers need unions?

John Dewey (1859-1952), one of the most important educational philosophers in the twentieth century, was a staunch advocate of unionizing the teaching profession--he held membership card number 1 in the American Federation of Teachers. Seeing education as a social force, and teachers as the spearheads of the action, he believed organized labor could only benefit the teaching class and education itself.

Undoubtedly, organized labor is extremely important in any area of work in which a high number of people make a living. When the line of work affects individual and social development as education does, then unions are not only a necessity but a mandatory requirement. They ward off arbitrary decisions by the bureaucrats of education, keep lawmakers on their toes, promote lobbying efforts to avoid or reverse controversial measures, among numerous other services to union members in particular and the community interest in general.

Indeed, there is the need for an active organization to represent the interests of teachers; professional and otherwise. As Dewey once stressed, "in representing them (teachers), it represents also the protection of the children and the youth in the schools against all of the outside interests, economic and political and others, that would exploit the schools for their own ends." In fact, when teachers are empowered by a network of peers committed to protecting the interests of all, they are more likely to focus on the academic and social responsibilities of their profession without fear of retaliation. This is why tenure is a most crucial issue in the teaching profession.

Unfortunately, like any other bureaucracy, unions become independent entities with interests of their own. But as long as they remain organizations to protect their members' professional interests, they are the most precious resource in the labor movement. Otherwise they can be a hindrance.

Occasionally, education unions align themselves with business interests, public officials, labor and community leaders, parents and a misled public opinion in order to build their appearance as leading national voices. In this instance, they do a disservice to both their members and education itself. By taking such a stance, they become pawns on the chess board of education for economic functionalism. They establish rules and demand, in the name of all their membership, stronger curricula, better standardized test results, high standards for teacher certification (though it is not clear what this means), among other travesties of education for economic functions. After all, as a former president of the American Federation of Teachers once stated, " unions will be out of business if they don't convince a skeptical public that the work they do is for the good of public education."

On the other hand, some teachers, albeit inconspicuously, resent certain union policies and rules. One particular teacher in New York, while acknowledging her union's effort in obtaining "wonderful benefits and decent salaries," added an additional comment: "Union rules should be there to protect us, not prevent us from doing innovative things."

Indeed, teachers do need unions; not only to protect teachers' professional interests, but to support pioneer initiatives in the reform of education. They must be organizations of teachers, by teachers for teachers.

What is the nominal (and real) value of teachers?

The theory of supply and demand, one of the most fundamental theories of the dominant economic system, contends that the value of a commodity is determined by its demand in relation to its supply in the marketplace. However, when it comes to the teaching class, this theory blatantly contradicts its principles. How can a labor-commodity in extremely high demand and critical short supply have such a low average market value in salary rates?

Despite the fact that education is a multi-billion dollar industry of paramount importance to the economic, social and political development of the nation, teachers are one of the lowest paid professionals with college degrees. In fact, society is willing to pay more for the labor of plumbers and mechanics--who generally do not have a college degree--than to compensate the invaluable work of teachers accordingly. If it weren't enough to generate resentment among the members of the teaching class, people are more readily inclined to complain, criticize, blame and judge the work of teachers than they would their plumbers ormechanics.

Besides being underpaid, teachers do not only carry out their educational functions in the classroom, they also are called upon to be supervisors, custodians, counselors, cafeteria monitors, coaches, among other menial extra curricular activities. No wonder the burnout rate among teachers in our nation is so high--often affecting the best and most dedicated professionals.

When we compare the data of entry level wages among professions in recent years, teachers have a dismal placing. According to a U.S. News & World Report survey, the average annual entry level salary for teachers on the west coast of the United States (California, Nevada, Idaho, Oregon and Washington) in 1993 was approximately $1,000 higher than the entry level salary of a janitor, $800 less than a security guard, and $1,400 less than a secretary. This information clearly--and sadly--reveals the value that our society bestows upon the profession that makes all other professions possible. It is ironic that a professional class of unmatched importance to economic, political, social and individual development is so meagerly compensated.

In addition to disregarding the financial value of the teacher in the marketplace, the low social value conferred to the profession is truly disturbing. Mortimer J. Adler (1902-   ), the great American philosopher and educator has remarked that "not only we pay teachers too little for work they are expected to do, we also fail in this country to give them the respect that the worth of their service to their community deserves." This lack of respect and appreciation for the teaching profession is present in everyday situations.

A few years ago the national media published a story of a dispute over a building elevator between a famous professional tennis player and an elderly retired teacher. As the dispute escalated, the professional athlete was reported to have allegedly said: "Who the hell are you? I know who you are. You're a lousy school teacher." Although this is a particular example, it certainly resonates a social lack of estimation for one of the most honorable professions in the world. And yet, in tennis analogy, on the court of importance to individual and social development, teachers easily ace professional athletes out of the match, though the latter are the ones who collect the prize money and have the bragging rights to insult.

As the nominal and real value of the teaching profession contradict each other, the teacher gradually grows aware and tired of not being appreciated and compensated according to her market value. Add to it stressful situations with the bureaucracy of education, overcrowded classrooms, dangerous working conditions-- no longer limited to inner city schools, as massacres in middle class schools have evinced--and we have a group of much needed professionals burning out in every level: physically, emotionally, spiritually and financially. This most critical crisis in education seems to be oblivious to the bureaucrats of the educational system.

Like the slave-teacher in Ancient Greece and the servant-teacher in modern European history, the social and financial status of teachers today remain despicably low. It is time to restore some prestige to the profession. Waiting for recognition, however, will only aggravate our frustration, for it will not come effortlessly. It is our responsibility to reclaim the acknowledgement we duly deserve.

Why do teachers need summers off?

One of the most controversial issues in the debate of teachers' compensation and benefits is summer vacations. It has also been used as an argument for those proponents of low salaries, claiming that teachers actually work only nine months a year. Only nine months a year? Let's see.

Only people who have worked with children on a daily basis know how challenging and demanding the task can be. Plus, if the adult in charge is genuinely concerned with the human development of the child, the undertaking becomes even more difficult, for raising a child in freedom of thought, emotions and expression is infinitely more exhausting than educating for conformity. The former takes energy, effort and dedication, while the latter only requires the educator to follow the narrow rules.

Except for the duration of time in which the teacher is engaged in the educational process of a child, her commitment is not with one or even a few individuals per se, but with the responsibility to assist in the guidance of human development. This idiosyncrasy of the teaching profession gives the class a very peculiar role in the education of the individual: a surrogate parent, partially and temporarily responsible for the development of numerous children in the course of a career. Someone whose responsibility is so elevated must be assured to be balanced in mind, heart and spirit; otherwise there is substantial risk for failure and severe social consequences.

Therefore teachers must be spared of working long hours and full years.

However, if common sense does not suffice to convince the skeptical public, then let's substantiate the reasoning with facts. Teachers do an extraordinary amount of work on their own time--evenings, weekends, and, of course, summers. Besides having to prepare classes, correct tests and homework projects, confer with parents and colleagues after hours (often on the phone at home), teachers are also required to attend committee and faculty meetings, professional development training, and even participate in extra-curricular activities, such as coaching, journalism club, etc. All of this leads to intense overall fatigue and irritable nerves that corrode the joy of teaching; a terrible outcome for the interests of students and education as a whole.

In addition to the fundamental need for a shorter work-year, the educational system would be much better served if teachers were assured a sabbatical year every eight years of continuous work; a practice Waldorf Schools have been employing very successfully. University professors are endowed with this privilege based on the "need" to do research, though many do not use this time for the intended purpose. But why teachers who work with students in the most difficult, challenging and important stage of human development are not granted the same professional benefit as their counterpart in the field of education? In reality, this should not even be considered a direct benefit for the individual teacher but a boon to the educational system itself.

Sponsoring conditions that support the educator in his natural love of teaching is one of the best antidotes to the massive evasion of teachers. Therefore a sabbatical year is a favorable recourse, if not to eliminate altogether, at least to appease the crisis in education.

Do teachers need to have an ontological vocation? (the genuine license)

The educational system today has turned into a utilitarian training system in which technicians of education are trained to operate the complex information machinery. Lost somewhere in this process is the notion and understanding of ontological vocation.

It was the Brazilian educator Paulo Freire (1921-1997) who originated the term ontological vocation. The word ontological means "relating to or studying the nature of existence." In Freirean terminology it refers to a natural proclivity to act and transform the world on behalf of a fuller and richer life; individually and collectively. When it comes to teaching, ontological vocation is imperative to quality education for human development. If imbued with this natural talent, the teacher can be a beacon of light in the life of a child, as well as a tremendous asset to social development.

So, is ontological vocation in education a necessary principle of a good teacher? Absolutely! It is from the core of this natural element that the three most important requisites for quality teaching emerge: love of teaching, love of learning and love of children. Unfortunately, in our utilitarian educational system, the training of teachers is what determines the authentication and licensure of the professional; even if the individual chooses the career as a sheer means of making a living. Meanwhile, a plethora of competent, loving and bona fide educators whose only license is their ontological vocation, are barred from being of service to education in public schools. Since they are often times in disagreement with the methodology of utilitarian education--the fact they did not pursue a license through the traditional channels can be seen as evidence of their refutation--they automatically become *persona non grata* in the industry of automation and conformity.

Undoubtedly, the most fundamental aspect that should determine the eligibility of a teacher to teach in public schools, or in any other educational setting for that matter, is ontological vocation. It is the foundation upon which all other requisites for the teaching profession should be based.

Can teachers really be a source of transformational action?

There are two distinctive manners in which teachers can carry out their daily work: they can teach for freedom or they can teach for conformity and domestication. The former is characterized by the responsibility of teaching and the latter by the duty of teaching. The difference lies in the fact that responsibility evokes the notion of freedom, whereas duty relates to an obligation possibly bereft of free-will.

A considerable number of teachers fall in the duty category, as they were properly trained to be in schools of education. While fulfilling this passive function, the pseudo-educator acts as a technician who ensures that the political, economic and moral *status quo* is duly nurtured in young minds. They work in such automatic fashion, that they unwittingly ignore the sociological, psychological, emotional and spiritual components of education. Instead of being moved by an ontological vocation and sincere desire to promote integral human development, these well-trained technicians of information become appendages of an educational industry dedicated to the production and consumption of data--and goods.

Fortunately, there also are a great number of teachers who place their responsibility over their duty. They are guided by a calling that overrides any and all bureaucratic obligations of their chosen profession. The focus of their daily work is on human development in freedom, not on the sheer preparation of their pupils for standardized tests, college entrance exams or a $uccessful professional career, though intellectual curiosity is not to be neglected. They are warriors on the battlefield of education, where the training of the workforce mode fights the unyielding human spirit crying out for a knowledge far beyond the limiting accumulation of data. This cadre of education professionals sets up the groundwork for transformational action in the individual and society. They are the unsung heroes of world history.

There also are known heroes who have proven that teachers can exert an extraordinary influence in the transformational action for a more just social order. Perhaps the most remarkable example of a teacher's participation in important historical events is the case of Simon Carreño Rodriguez. He was the most influential teacher of Simon Bolívar (1783-1830), known as "The Liberator of Spanish America." In fact, Rodriguez's influence was so profound, that it would not be farfetched to say that a teacher had an enormous participation in the independence movement of Spanish America. This has been documented in the words of Bolívar himself who wrote these words about his teacher: "You formed my heart for liberty, for justice, for the great, for beautiful...You cannot imagine how deeply your lessons impressed themselves into my heart. Always present before my intellectual eyes I have followed them as infallible guides."

There are a number of other well-known teachers who have profoundly changed the lives of their famous pupils and the world; e.g., Socrates and Plato, Plato and Aristotle, Anne Sullivan and Helen Keller, among many others. There also are many teachers who, inconspicuously, make a tremendous difference in education for human development every day they go to work. They are professionals who constantly prove that teachers can, indeed, be powerful contributors to positive social change.

In this light, the responsibility of the teaching profession demands an education based on critical thinking in freedom. It is the only insurance against dogma and indoctrination that have assailed the educational system in the past two centuries.

What is the future of the teaching profession?

The future of the teaching profession is an enigma in this rapidly expanding electronic age. As technology develops at an astounding pace, the likelihood that education will rely more on computers than on human educators seems frighteningly feasible. Indeed, the idea of mechanistic teachers using mechanistic tools to prepare students for a mechanistic society is a nightmare of Orwellian proportion.

On the opposite side of the spectrum, the dream version of education, teachers use their influential power to make sure the profession steers toward a diverse educational process that promotes integral human development. An education in which every child has the inviolable right to a completely fulfilling childhood, free from the materialistic pressures of the economic-educational machinery. An education in which schools, instead of being a center of training and information consumption, are genuine temples of learning.

Somewhere between the dream and the nightmare lies the future of education. It is up to each individual teacher to determine, regardless of the circumstances of the system, if he wants to live an educational dream or a nightmare; and which cause she is willing to favor and work for. In the end, it is a matter of personal choice--one of immense responsibility.

PART II

"One had only to cram all this stuff into one's mind, whether one liked it or not. This coercion had such a deterring effect that, after I had passed the final examination, I found the consideration of any scientific problems distasteful to me for an entire year...It is in fact nothing short of a miracle that the modern methods of instruction have not yet entirely strangled the holy curiosity of inquiry; for this delicate little plant, aside from stimulation, stands mainly in need of freedom; without this it goes to wrack and ruin without fail."

Albert Einstein

"We may very well manage to teach a few more million children how to read and write; but we will not have solved the overarching problem of a technological competence gone wild, a scientific expertise gone mad, an intellectual excellence that does not even dare to state or specify what master it will serve."

Jonathan Kozol

THE EDUCATIONAL SYSTEM

What is education for?

Etymologically, the word education comes from the Latin word educatio and the verb educare, which essentially means the act to create, to guide and to conduct. But that is in terms of semantics. Some modern educators might argue that education is the art of learning the utilization of knowledge.

Since Ancient Greece, education has been one of the most powerful social forces responsible for forging Western civilization. It has also been a fundamental tool of domination, often manipulated by economic-political structures (empires, states, religions, etc.) for their own specific interests and objectives. Moreover, the historical process of education has been marked almost exclusively by intellectual and technical development, while little attention--mostly through the Humanities--has been devoted to the complex development of the human being.

After the fall of the Roman Empire, Scholasticism emerged sustained by the central idea that reason and faith were compatible; a shrewd maneuver to rationalize the dogma of the Church. It was not until the Renaissance period that the supremacy of Scholasticism was confronted, followed by the economic development of the

New World, which opened up educational opportunities once reserved exclusively for the clergy, nobility and the ruling class. However, it was the advent of the Industrial Revolution that forever altered the meaning, goals and purpose of education. It turned education into economic functionalism.

The Industrial Revolution triggered an education revolution in itself, for the unremitting technological development and economic expansion demanded a "production" of qualified labor in "factory schools." Consequently, mathematics, sciences, technical and vocational education became pivotal to the sustenance of the new economic order, and still prevail today. Thus, the economic function of the individual (laborer/consumer) superseded his human developmental needs; i.e., intellectual, cultural, emotional and spiritual knowledge.

Today, the Industrial Revolution has merged with the Electronic Revolution, and in this process, education reform is defined in a materialist conception of education in which education is geared toward the acquisition of specific knowledge to fulfill economic functions.

Nevertheless, the verb educare (the act to create, to guide and to conduct) has not changed its meaning, only the objective of its use has been distorted. The verb that was originally intended to guide the development of humanity has turned into the foundation of a system that promotes economic development. Although there is nothing particularly wrong with education for economic development, the excessive focus of education on this area, in detriment to some fundamental needs of human development, is not only a travesty but an irresponsibility of the educational system, especially when we face unprecedented challenges in the new millennium.

Perhaps we have lost track of the meaning of knowledge and we no longer know what education is supposed to be. Therefore, in order to find out what education is, we must first understand the meaning of knowledge and its relationship to education.

What does Knowledge mean?

Knowledge is not something that is made, finished and transferred. It is not concrete and absolute in nature either. Even the dictionary does not clearly define the meaning of knowledge. The Merriam Webster's Collegiate Dictionary, Tenth Edition, defines knowledge as "the fact or condition of knowing something, being aware of something, the range of one's information or understanding, the fact or condition of having information or being learned." However, it never specifies what the information or understanding referring to knowledge is, or how it distinguishes itself from information and understanding. Inferentially, knowledge is an abstract concept that varies according to the nature and objectives of the observer.

In relation to education, however, we must attempt to define knowledge in order to establish educational goals. The investigation ought to begin with the theory of knowledge (a major branch of philosophy), which establishes the general nature of knowledge involving the subject (the knower) and the object (the known). Since the former is the foundation upon which the latter will be placed, self-knowledge should be the first step toward comprehensive knowledge linked to information and understanding. Thus, the Delphic motto "know thyself," the mainspring of all psychology, should also be the motto of an educational system genuinely concerned with human development.

However, since the mechanistic conception of René Descartes (1596-1650), knowledge and education have been perceived according to the maxim "Cogito, ergo sum," (I think, therefore I am). This Cartesian mentality has limited the scope of knowledge to intellectual activity bereft of any emotional and spiritual content, for according to Descartes, thinking is what defines one's existence.

Such a lopsided mentality is greatly responsible for the current crisis in education. It has also created much distress to human societies, while engendering an imbalance in human nature. Moreover, the separation of reason from all the other aspects of the human complexity has generated twofold calamities: it has annihilated the individual from her multifaceted wholeness, and has monopolized knowledge to the interests of science, as though it were the only function of its existence. The knowledge conveyed in public schools is based on this obsolete principle of intellectual dominance.

Except for some alternative education, guiding children in a process of self-discovery and self-knowledge (the know thyself maxim referred above) is virtually non-existent. Teaching children to develop their emotions, compassion, sympathy, empathy, cooperation, a sense of community and union with all that live and exist is often regarded as a futile educational endeavor. They are not considered important skills in a highly competitive marketplace. Besides, there are no required standardized test to measure these "superfluous" attributes.

While the Cartesian mentality maintains the idea of knowledge as food for thought, it neglects the emotional and spiritual elements of human nature as water for the soul. Both are absolutely critical for educational development, just as much as food and water are indispensable to the human body.

As we can see, there is much more to knowledge than mathematical equations, scientific theories and accumulation of general information. There is a knowledge that does not happen in the intellect but in the heart and soul of the human being; a knowledge that assists in the process of self-awareness, which in turn transforms the acquisition of information and experiences into wisdom--the zenith of knowing. But as long as reason remains divorced from the other equally important components of the human complexity, the educational system will continue to be a debacle, even if it could achieve perfect standardized test results worldwide, for the imbalance in human development would persist.

Thus, reforming education is inextricably intertwined with a new concept of knowledge. It must redefine itself in what it is and for what purpose, considering the circumstantial needs of humanity at a particular historical time.

Why should we implement a new concept of knowledge in education?

In order to answer this question, it is important to start with an evaluation of the current world situation at the dawn of a new millennium.

Despite the extraordinary technological achievements in the twentieth century--which people are so enthralled with that they fail to grasp the reality around them--the problems assailing humanity at this time are unparalleled to any other challenge we have ever faced in human history. (Uncontrolled population explosion that only aggravates the unremitting depletion of natural resources in an ever-expanding economic system.) Plus, ecological disasters, widespread and growing poverty, physical and mental health crisis (chronic depression, AIDS, recurrence of deadly diseases, etc.), senseless violence and hate crimes are but a few symptoms of an extremely troubled humanity. These are some of the serious issues the children of today will have to deal with tomorrow on a much larger scale.

Nevertheless, people are naively dazzled with the scientific, technological and economic achievements of modern society, while closing their eyes to an ugly reality they do not want to see.

This bleak scenario is in the foreground of the educational system, though it seems oblivious to the bureaucrats whose primary concerns are the exclusive interests of economic functions. As long as the standardized test results reveal positive answers, why bother to propel students and teachers to question reality? Perhaps because they don't know that the learned person is not the one who gives the right answers, but the one who asks the right questions. And the time to ask the right questions is now!

A new concept of knowledge is imperative to an education reform that envisions the ultimate good in human development. This process must begin with guidance to self-knowledge and awareness of the universal challenges that life presents to everyone. Who has ever been taught in schools about the inevitability of death, the emotional pain caused by separation, the trials of sickness, among many other circumstances of life that characterize the human experience. Aren't these issues of paramount importance in the educational process of a child, since he will certainly experience them sooner or later in his life? And please don't tell us that this is the responsibility of the church, for the church does not teach awareness, it mostly indoctrinates and consoles. The challenges of life are to be presented in a philosophical-spiritual manner that empowers the individual while enhancing his knowledge of life itself.

The reformed educational system should be founded upon the dialectical relationship between knowledge and learner; that is, knowledge exists according to the needs (other than pragmatic) of the learner who assimilates it. In this approach, education should be carried out according to the student's particular interests, rather than the demands of economic functionalism. As it is, freedom of learning is non-existent; on the contrary, schooling has become an oppressive coercive force that utilizes knowledge as its main tool of oppression.

Perhaps a "trinity of knowledge" could establish the foundation of a new educational system: the development of Mind (intellect), Heart (emotions) and Spirit (the evolving human as a species). This approach would promote self-knowledge, social knowledge, and, ultimately, wisdom. In self-knowledge the individual asserts her existence in the world. In social knowledge he learns that he is not only in the world but with the world and everyone else in it. And it is from the harmonious integration of self-knowledge and social knowledge that knowledge itself expands--and wisdom is born.

What remains to be determined is how to integrate a new concept of knowledge into an educational system geared toward economic functionalism.

How can transformational education be introduced?

Once the realization of the need for a new approach to knowledge in education has been determined, the next step is to establish an educational program that will promote this new strategy for human development. This process begins with an absolute understanding that there is something terribly wrong with the way education has been conducted hitherto. It is a distorted vision of the purpose of education in human life.

A new concept of knowledge that considers the concomitant educational development of Mind, Heart and Spirit, could be introduced using a method that has already been proven successful in a pedagogy of freedom and liberation.

The Brazilian educator Paulo Freire perfected a method for teaching illiterates by linking literacy to the development of critical social consciousness. Based on the acceptance of the student as a Subject rather than an object in the educational process, he viewed the individual as a creator, re-creator and transformer of his cultural reality (this is what he called "man's ontological vocation"). He also believed, and I concur, that one of the most critical objectives of education should be the re-humanization of a dehumanized society. This is precisely what a new concept of knowledge is all about: re-humanization.

Taking the Freirean approach of critical consciousness, students' critical thinking can be stimulated in a creative process of self-discovery, while igniting the awareness of the circumstances of life around them. As they gradually develop their intellect, emotions and inner spirituality in relation to their fellow-humans and the world, they are likely to become aware that modernization (technological, scientific and economic expansion) and development (what is reflected in what has become of the individual, society and the environment) are very distinct concepts that deserve critical scrutiny. They will be able to discern the pros and cons of their own educational process, the consequences of unbridled consumerism, and if the price they pay is really worth it.

No wonder Paulo Freire was vehemently rejected by

the powers-that-be before becoming a quasi-mythological character in the area of philosophy of education around the world. His is a pedagogy of transformation of the human spirit; and that is exactly what we need the most nowadays.

Hence, provided with the proper educational tools, both teachers and students can gradually discern their inner and surrounding realities, and deal with them in a transformational critical manner. However, a vehicle in which to conduct and facilitate this process is necessary.

What can be used to carry out transformational education?

As human life becomes more and more centralized in the economic objectives of production and consumption, the human spirit seems to be gradually withering. The evidence to this fact is clearly shown in the increasing number of individuals suffering from some sort of mental illness (one in every five Americans are considered to be mentally ill), ranging from mild depression to utter insanity. According to the American Psychiatric Association, there currently are more than 300 kinds of mental disorders, compared to only 22 in 1918. A substantial number of individuals afflicted by these mental disorders are highly $uccessful white collar professionals.

Seemingly, the educational system has been contributing to this madness through unnecessary academic pressures that create immense stress in the developing child. The case of the famous British philosopher John Stuart Mill (1806-1873) illustrates this argument quite well. His father James Mill elaborated a comprehensive educational program that began with Greek and arithmetic at the age of three. By the age of twelve he had studied Euclid and algebra, the Greek and Latin poets, and was introduced to logic in Aristotle's Organon and the Latin scholastic manuals on the subject. At the age of twenty, however, he was on the verge of severing relations with his father and was overcome by a depression which lasted for several years. In more moderate terms, the modern educational system does to our children what James Mill did to his.

One possible way to remedy this problem is to bring about a Humanities program in combination with Freirean methodology. The goal is to transform the mechanistic educational system into a humanistic educational development in which humankind, not the economic system, is the ultimate beneficiary of the educational process. We could call it the Humanities Revolution in which the three fundamental elements that constitute human knowledge (mind, heart and spirit) are fully integrated and developed accordingly.

Because the educational system is committed to economic functions, education has become one-sided with excessive emphasis given to mathematics, science, technology and other pragmatic disciplines. Immersed in this process, people have lost touch with themselves, their fellow-citizens, their environment and even with life itself. Worse yet, people seem to be losing the capacity for meaningful emotional experiences. Ultimately, we have been producing sick people in order to have a healthy economy.

It is the role of the Humanities Revolution to call for a counterbalance in the traditional schooling dominated by science and technology. Then, learning would be regulated by the disciplines of the Humanities and for the purpose of serving humanity. In the end, the individual, society, and even the economic system itself would benefit from this educational venture. In fact, J. Paul Getty (1892-1976), one of the wealthiest and shrewdest businessman in America, was a staunch advocate of the value of the Humanities in the business world. In his book *How to Be a Successful Executive* he wrote: "I do not hesitate to state flatly that I consider my liberal-arts education to have had far greater overall importance than any of the purely technical or professional subjects I studied." Nevertheless, the prevalence of the so-called useful disciplines still hinders the proliferation of the Humanities in education.

It is important to heed the perils that a technology-dominated society without fully developed individuals poses to civilization. In two classics of world literature, Aldous Huxley's *Brave New World* and George Orwell's *1984*, the writers depicted a society dominated by technological apparatus controlling mind-conditioned individuals. When these books were published (1932 and 1949, respectively), it seemed like a farfetched situation only imaginable in the fertile minds of creative artists. Today, however, as we look back to the twentieth century, we can clearly see that it was a time characterized by astounding technological and scientific progress, totalitarian regimes, and brain-washing propaganda glorifying the myths of divergent political and economic orders. What a few decades ago was perceived as science-fiction, it is rapidly becoming a frightening reality.

As the great German playwright and poet Bertolt Brecht (1898-1956) once stated, "art is not a mirror to reflect reality, but a hammer with which to shape it." Indeed, great art can be revolutionary because it not only affects the individual, but compels her to question reality. No wonder artists from all kinds of artistic expression (writers, painters, filmmakers, etc.) have been persecuted during turbulent times in the twentieth century; e.g., the Bolshevik Revolution, the Spanish Civil War, the Communist witch hunting of the McCarthy era in the United States, to name a few. In fact, it is astonishing that art has not been entirely banned or forbidden throughout history by the oppressing ruling powers. Although they have not gone that far yet, they have managed to suppress the artistic spirit through both pseudo-morality and a technologically oriented educational agenda. Take for example the case of a school in the state of Virginia in which the entire Humanities program was eliminated in order to siphon the funds to create and operate a computer lab.

In addition to obliterating the Humanities program on behalf of pragmatic disciplines that benefit economic interests, the bureaucrats of education and their lackeys have managed to convince the public that music, dance, theater and the arts in general are fluffs and frills of educational programs. Evidently, they are well-aware of the transformational power of the arts, and therefore do not want to incur any risks to their conformist molding programs.

Henceforth, a reformative educational program aimed at integral human development must begin with a renaissance of the Humanities; not only in schools but in society at large.

Whose invisible hand controls the educational system?

From kindergarten to graduate school, education is a multi-billion dollar industry. Considering the high caliber of this business and the extraordinary impact it has on economic development, it is obvious that the educational system is a very well-safeguarded institution. But by whom?

We can dilute the question of whose invisible hand controls the educational system by eliminating those who certainly do not: teachers, students, parents and the general public obviously do not. Neither do scholars, scientists and researchers. We might be tempted to say that the Department of Education is the organization in charge of the education machinery. Possibly in charge but certainly not in control. That brings us back to the original question.

Seemingly, the most obvious possibility of controlling forces after this elimination process are economic interests under the auspices of political structures. After all, not only does the business of education generate billions of dollars in profits, when not exercised in freedom, it is a powerful tool for manipulation of ideas. In fact, it has been cunningly utilized by both dictatorial and democratic nations in the pursuit of ideological indoctrination.

Another aspect must be considered: freedom in education can be one of the most viable threats to a failed social system of values, for it leads to critical thinking, dialogue, debate and, eventually, action. What happened at the University of California at Berkeley in the 1960's is a classical example of freedom in education in action. However, the movement was immediately repressed in a manner that was the antithesis to the moral written covenant of freedom, justice and democratic values. It became evident that the powerful forces that control the educational system would not tolerate freedom of expression that was not conducive to the interests of the *status quo*.

There should be no room for skepticism regarding education as an industry manipulated by powerful economic and political forces. Obviously, the invisible hand controlling the educational system is the same hand choking teachers and students--not to mention the environment--out of breath. In spite of the asphyxiation, the movement for freedom in education perseveres.

What should determine the direction of education?

The answer to this question is intrinsically related to the idea of what kind of person we wish to produce. If public education continues to be a factory for the training of the workforce, rather than emphasizing the legitimate educational rights for human development, then we already know what determines the direction of education.

Perhaps there once was a time when education could have been equated with training, accumulation of facts and information, among other exclusively intellectual activities. But times have changed. What once was can no longer be. The unprecedented challenges we face in the twenty-first century have transformed, dramatically, the dynamics of the role and purpose of education. While before (up to the first half of the twentieth century) it was bearably possible to maintain education at a utilitarian level, the current crisis in the human situation demands a different kind of education. It can no longer remain a passive and diligent participant in the training of the workforce and the docile citizen program. Education must become the catalyst in the difficult task of rehumanizing a social (dis)order gone berserk.

Ultimately, what should determine the direction of education is human need. Although we have various necessities, both individually and collectively, it is crucial to prioritize them according to their degree of importance at a particular time or situation. Considering the circumstances of our time, it is conclusively clear that preparing students to fulfill economic functions should not be a top priority; not when integral human development has reached its nadir at the apex of technological progress.

As the misdirected educational system goes astray on the path of economic functionalism, perhaps it is time to re-evaluate its aim and take the road less traveled by; it can make all the difference.

What is the aim of education?

In his book *The Aims of Education*, distinguished British philosopher Alfred North Whitehead (1861-1947) averred that the entire book was a protest against dead knowledge. He vehemently contended that scraps of information have nothing to do with comprehensive and meaningful education; on the contrary, they were what he called "inert ideas;" that is to say, ideas that are merely received into the mind without being utilized, or tested. In fact, he claimed that education with inert ideas is not only useless but it is harmful. He finally reminds us that the most valuable intellectual development is self-development.

Although Whitehead is a prominent figure in Western intellectual thinking, his observations in the field of education don't seem to have been taken very seriously. Not only is the educational system characterized by inert ideas, it also reflects several other inert effects that do not benefit the development of the individual. Consequently, neither the faculty of reasoning nor feeling is able to develop properly when they are mutually exclusive in the educational process.

As it is today, the aim of education is to produce a well-trained group of individuals for the job-market. But urgent problems require urgent measures, therefore we must shift the aim of education toward the study of the problems at the core of the current human crisis. But as long as education remains submissive to the demands of economic and political forces, the aim of education will continue to be a mechanistic "banking system," as Paulo Freire described, in which the well-trained bank-clerk teachers deposit data in the memory bank of students. The teacher, though well-intentioned, does an enormous disservice to his pupils by failing to perceive that the deposits themselves contain contradictions about reality. Thus, the teacher contributes to enhancing the passive role of utilitarian education, while her students starve for meaningful knowledge. It is inert ideas in action.

The aim of education per se is determined by the prevalent forces and interests controlling it. In the past the Jesuits did a remarkable job ensuring the absolute sovereignty of the educational system, while using pupils as pawns in the interests of the Church. Many other cultural groups and institutions have done the same. At this time, the invisible hand controlling education is attached to the production body; an economic system that insatiably demands higher consumption in direct connection with incessant and ever-escalating production. This is a ramification of the State itself, which vitally depends on the educational system as ideological validation for its policies and procedures. The genuine educator, however, should be more committed to the individual human interests of her students than the selfish interests of the State, Church or any other institution.

Undoubtedly, these are times of great angst. While the economic prosperity of (a few) nations and individuals expands, so do the numerous problems uncontrolled development creates. As the problems augment in concomitant relation to population explosion, a world overcrowded with people in fear is a recipe for disaster. Therefore one of the main priorities of education today ought to be the teaching of learning to live without fear, while guiding youngsters through the rehumanization and rebuilding process of a more humanly civilized world. It is a long and arduous path; but one that will lead us out of the maze of confusion and self-destruction.

In the end, as Whitehead proclaimed, there is only one subject matter for education, and that is Life in all its manifestations.

What is the role of religion (Spirituality) in education?

Religion is, perhaps, the most controversial subject in human culture. Once individuals establish a belief system involving deities, worship and rituals, and draft a covenant of precepts to which a social group commits to, religion has been created. When different groups and cultures form conflicting belief systems, religious contention inevitably occurs.

From Animism to Polytheism to Monotheism, humanity has had a myriad of religious experiences in search of Truth. But if we carefully observe the patterns of religious behavior and the circumstances that propel them, we will realize that the soul of religion is not the pursuit of Truth per se but a strong drive ignited by the human condition, e.g., insecurity, loneliness, death and several emotions spawned from fear. Hence, considering the vast religious possibilities (there are dictionaries of world religions and encyclopedia of gods), the interference of any religion in the educational process of a young child can be an affront to his freedom to learn. Unless taught as an exclusive discipline of the Humanities, religion cannot serve education, only domestication.

The opinions about religion and its role in society are immensely diverse. Ambrose Bierce called religion "the daughter of Hope and Fear, explaining to ignorance the nature of the Unknowable." Sigmund Freud contended that "religious beliefs correspond closely with the phantasies of infantile life, mainly unconscious ones, concerning the sexual life of one's parents." Karl Marx understood religion as "the sigh of the oppressed creature, the heart of a heartless world, just as it is the spirit of a spiritless situation." And Alfred North Whitehead claimed that "religion is what the individual does with his own solitariness." In education, religion should be the pursuit of spirituality in freedom; utterly bereft of indoctrination.

Religion seems to be a vital survival mechanism for humanity. However, because religion and ethics are so closely related, they can blend into each other confusing the discernment of which is which. Therefore it is imperative to distinguish the two in any particular context.

Another discernment that is equally important to make is that of religion and science. In the past they were intertwined and posed a threat to intellectual freedom and human development. The case of Galileo Galilei (1564-1642), who had to recant his scientific discoveries before the Church in order to stay alive; and Giordano Bruno (1548-1600), the martyr of science, who was burned at the stake for heresy (he postulated the infinity of the universe and the truth of the Copernican hypothesis) are indelible testimonies to the dangers that religion in science represents. These institutions must remain independent from each other if they are to serve the interests of human development.

In the same way that religion blends with ethics and, occasionally, with science, it also mingles with politics. The latter mix can be so intricate and dangerous that The Constitution of the United States explicitly stresses the separation of Church and State in the First Amendment of the Bill of Rights.

As religion influences politics and vice-versa, it can be difficult to differentiate their mutually inclusive concerns. Consequently, a political-religious alliance ensues and the role of religion in education also fulfills specific political interests. This is clearly observable in the political scenario in the United States, where powerful religious groups have an extraordinary influence in the policies of national administration. The overt alliance between the Christian Coalition and the Republican Party endorses this argument.

Riding the wave of religious activities, politics has created an indoctrination pattern that is quasi-religious itself--and omnipresent in the educational system. The "religious dogma of politics" invokes the ideals of freedom and justice for all, devotional patriotism, righteousness; all cleverly cloaked under the theoretical principles of free-market economy and democracy, as though they were interdependent. These theories are shoved into the developing mind and emotional body of youngsters without any consideration to their critical thinking. We do not even give them the opportunity to evaluate by themselves how these theories are, if at all, applicable to the reality they experience and observe. Nonetheless, it is socially acceptable to inculcate patriotism, as long as nobody attempts to discuss its surreptitious purpose.

The religious-political pact in the educational system reveals itself in the Pledge of Allegiance to the flag in our schools. Originally written in 1892 by Frank Bellamy, a nationalist and member of The Society of Christian Socialists, the Pledge of Allegiance, when uttered routinely as a mere sense of duty, promotes a false, passive and superficial form of patriotism--more like mind and emotional-conditioning. It is, indeed, a subtle form of political indoctrination. Incidentally, it is opportune to observe that in Nazi Germany the salutation of the flag was a notorious strategy to validate Hitler's program of national pride and mass-destruction; and by the way, before the dictatorship, Germany was a democratic state.

However, the worst set back of the Pledge of Allegiance is the smothering of critical thinking, for children will not question the zeal of their emotions with conflicting critical analysis. Besides, if the Ku Klux Klan and other extremist religious and political groups dutifully perform the salutation to the flag in their racist and dogmatic rituals, in a child's innocent mind, they must represent righteous and patriotic groups of citizens. In pedagogical terms, we can call it the promotion of ignorance through association.

The association of politics and religion grew stronger during the Cold War, mostly to join forces against the "communist godless states." First the United States Congress officially recognized the Pledge of Allegiance on December 28, 1945, just a few months after the end of World War II. A few years later, God became an important element in the propaganda strategy against the "evil empire;" thus by an Act of Congress in 1954, the original Pledge of Allegiance was changed from "one nation under my flag" to "one nation under God." This is a typical example of proselytization of politics that has a direct impact on education.

As the crisis in education flows along the disturbing motion of social chaos, professional politicians and religious leaders with political interests (a reminder that the founder of the Christian Coalition has vigorously pursued the highest political post in the world) have been emphasizing the role of religion in education. They encourage praying in schools, they call for the Ten Commandments to be posted in classrooms, and they make a big ado about not teaching Darwin's theory of evolution to students as if it were a heresy to be condemned--remember what happened to Giordano Bruno? In the end, it is all based on dogma and fear; and neither one has a place in education for freedom.

The role of religion as an inspiring social force free from biases and dogmas is what spirituality in education should be. In spirituality, ethics is born from a comprehensive inner search for the beautiful, just and loving aspects of human nature, not a moral set of rules prescribed by the dominant culture. Thus, the role of religion in education is an important one, as long as it is absolutely free from any dogma or indoctrination.

As we have seen here, the politics of education and the politics of religion are akin in nature. Both are based on indoctrination (uncritical learning) rather than freedom in education (critical thinking). Both need to re-adjust to the needs and demands of human development at this critical juncture in the history of civilization.

What should be the role of technology in education?

Technology is a powerful transformational tool that exerts an extraordinary impact on culture, psychology, sociology and every major aspect of individual and social progress. There have been four major technological revolutions in human history: the Agricultural Revolution, the Scientific Revolution, the Industrial Revolution and the Electronic Revolution. The first one drastically transformed the cultural essence of societies, as nomadic herding groups permanently settled down to practice agriculture, eventually leading to the establishment of cities; a very complex technological system. The second, by undermining the authority and assumptions of the past, became one of the dominant factors in the development of modern civilization. The third deeply affected the nature of labor, production and consumption, as well as deteriorating the environment to unimaginable conditions. The fourth, however, has engendered an even more significant impact on the individual, culture and society: it has been changing human nature.

The computer is the shining jewel in the technology crown of the twentieth century. As the factory system typifies the expansion of industrialism, the computer symbolizes the pinnacle of intellectual achievement in the Electronic Revolution. The telephone, the wireless radio, the automobile and even the airplane did not produce the same level of bedazzlement that computer technology has. Indeed, it has dominated our lives and influenced our culture like no other technological device.

Consequently, as our lives become increasingly more dominated by technology, we must ask ourselves some very elementary questions: Has the overall quality of life been enhanced? Has the world become a safer and better place where the human species--and others--may thrive? Has technology been contributing to human development? These and many other questions must be raised and debated in schools if technology is going to play a significant role in education. Upcoming generations have the inalienable right to discuss, in a critical thinking manner, their future in the world of tomorrow. To deny them this opportunity is an egregious abuse of power.

It is crucial to emphasize that it is not technology per se that is the root of the problem; on the contrary, it can be an important tool for human development. But when technology is manipulated by economic and political forces in the pursuit of profit or domination, then it becomes a self-created leviathan that poses a plethora of risks to everyone; either through electronic control of life or alienation of the human experience.

A classical example that illustrates the argument that knowledge is not exclusively related to reasoning and intellectual development is the case of Dr. Theodore Kaczynski, also known as the Unabomber. An intellectual and highly educated individual, this deranged solitary scholar terrorized the United States with unwarranted assassinations of those he deemed to be the cohorts of a self-destructive technological society. He epitomizes the idea of an unbalanced individual whose extensive education was primarily concerned with the expansion of his intellectual ability, while his emotional and spiritual development were clearly neglected. Consequently, in spite of his academic achievements, the underdeveloped aspects of his humanity posed serious danger to society.

Notwithstanding the fact that his criminal actions were deplorable and reprehensible, the reasoning of his anger against industrial-technological society (described in the manuscript known as the *Unabomber Manifesto*) is uncomfortably agreeable with a substantial number of people. As historian Roger Lane said, "what's really distressing is that this alienated madman on the fringes of society is thinking longer and harder than the people who are supposed to be running things...And what's scary is that you find yourself nodding in agreement again and again. He's got a lot of things right."

The Unabomber case has ignited umpteen debates about the role of technology in modern society. However, there is certainly nothing wrong with technology itself; it is its use and abuse that causes many problems. In other words, it is the human factor that is faulty and in desperate need of adjustment.

Another element that seems to be neglected is the role of education in technological development and use; after all, it is education that allows technology to evolve in the first place. Therefore the question not only relates to the role of technology in education but vice-versa as well. If the educational system promoted technical knowledge concomitantly with integral human development, the abysmal gap that separates the mind from the heart would not exist; or at least not at the current critical level.

Being at the mercy of technology has proven to be a dangerous situation. The big ado about the so-called Y2K problem at the turn of the century has served to awaken the consciousness of many. Suddenly we realized that modern society is completely dependent on technology for its most elementary operations. We rely on it so desperately that technology has become the force propelling the complex socio-economic machinery. It has become the food and water nourishing modern civilization.

In addition to the technical problems that can truly wreak havoc in our society, the comprehensive electronic apparatus, ranging from cable television to the internet, bombards us with a speedy avalanche of information impossible to absorb--much less in a critical thinking manner. The danger, however, is that this information subtly dictates what we buy, how we live, where we stand on the important issues of the day, whom we vote for, among other fundamental directions of our lives. Unfortunately, these sources of information often have hidden agendas, therefore misleading an apathetic society infatuated with the technological wonders that dominates it. In this process, entertainment, news, opinion, politics and other information commodities become indistinguishable from one another. Consequently, it is the responsibility of teachers to help individual students to become intelligent consumers of information.

However, when it comes to education, the point is not to be only an intelligent information consumer but a producer of intelligent information. And this cannot possibly be achieved unless the whole of human intelligence (mind, heart and spirit) participates in the educational process of students.

Although it hasn't yet been determined how technology can participate in the education of emotional and spiritual elements of humanity (the main reason being the lack of interest hitherto), at least it can be used as a gauge for how committed--or not--we are to the development and well-being of all individuals in society. The evidence of such commitment is intrinsic to our willingness to make technology serve humanity above and beyond any other interest. In order to reach this level, some fundamental changes have to take place; not in technology itself but the human being wielding this tool.

Unfortunately, the bureaucrats of education have a different approach. Fascinated with the electronic brain, they associate education reform and improvement with the availability and use of technology in the classroom. This is the traditional educational vision for the twenty-first century schools. Meanwhile, misguided by this myopic vision, research shows that many teachers rank computer skills and media technology as more "essential" than the Humanities or debating social problems. In addition, several studies, many of which were conducted by private interest groups linked to the computer industry, have come out to persuade the government and the general public that computer skills and technology are indispensable to education reform. From a strictly economic point of view this is irrefutable. But from the human development stance this is a fallacy of the imagination. Besides economic functionalism, there is absolutely no evidence that computers enhance the learning experience of anyone.

Nevertheless, filling classrooms with computers is considered more important than raising teacher's salaries, reducing class size, improving school nutritional programs or any other aspect of education that sponsors human welfare. In spite of the fact that computers in the classroom will never replace a word of encouragement, a supportive eye contact, a broad smile in a radiant face, a laughter or a warm comforting hug, they remain on the top of the priority list. School boards love them because there is public support; poorly trained and unskilled teachers love them because they do not have to teach; children love them because they do not have to focus on classroom drudgery; and parents love them for the soothing feeling that their beloved children will be well-prepared to get a good job. The purpose of education or the ultimate interest of the child is not considered in this incoherent scale of values.

As learning becomes more dependent on computers, the need for an education for human development becomes more and more urgent. The contemporary student has entered an electronic era of learning how not to learn, not to think, not to feel, and ultimately, not to act. This is a catastrophic scenario for an education devoted to integral human development in freedom.

Only educated, developed and rehumanized individuals will be able to transform chaos into harmony; hatred into love; violence into peace. Only then technology will not be a threat but a blessing to the development of the human spirit and civilization.

What is the role of education in promoting peace?

In order to even consider answering this question, we must first attempt to define peace, for how we define peace influences what we have to say about it. Let's begin with a brief overlook of peace in the historical context.

Since the beginning of recorded history, peace has always been regarded as a blessing and its opposite, war, as a scourge. Yet, it is only since the end of the Middle Ages that philosophers and statesmen have reflected systematically on the problem of peace. Nevertheless, it was not until the beginning of the nineteenth century that attempts to establish worldwide international peace came about, when the Napoleonic Wars destroyed the balance of power that had been the foundation of international peace since the end of theMiddle Ages.

In the twentieth century, the issue of peace became more complex and infinitely more delicate. After experiencing two devastating world wars, which culminated with a technological war machinery capable of putting an end to life as we know it, humanity has tried to minimize the risks of self-annihilation through the establishment of international organizations to secure peace. As in the nineteenth century the aftermath of the Napoleonic Wars gave birth to the Holy Alliance, in the twentieth century, after World War I and World War II, the League of Nations and the United Nations were established respectively. However, it is important to stress that none of these organizations have been able to put international peace on a more secure basis.

Ostensibly, the definition of peace has been considerably skewed. While peace is associated with the absence of organized armed conflict (war), the latter mostly refers to violent physical aggression. This equivocation of semantics is the foundation for the oxymoron often read and heard in the news media following the end of a war: "peace keeping force;" as though it were possible to force peace onto anyone.

Defining peace is even more complicated. But regardless of what definition we accept as most appropriate, peace begins with each individual and extends outward to the group. Peace in an individual context represents a state of inner harmony and tranquillity, while collective peace is intrinsically related to social justice; and in economic terms, that means a fair distribution of wealth among individuals and nations of the world. Thus, when it comes to individuals or countries, existing structures that ensure the rich to get richer while the poor gets poorer are committing a blatant act of violence against peace. In fact, this position has been endorsed by UNESCO (United Nations Educational, Scientific, and Cultural Organization) in its Second Medium-Term Plan, 1984-1989, Chapter 12, p.259:

"There can be no genuine peace when the most elementary human rights are violated or while situations of injustice continue to exist...Peace is incompatible with malnutrition and extreme poverty...The only lasting peace is a just peace based on respect for human rights. Furthermore, a just peace calls for the establishment of an equitable international order."

Before proceeding with the question of the role of education in promoting peace, I would like to suggest my allegorical definition of peace: Peace is the offspring of the holy matrimony of Love and Justice. When Love and Justice join together, peace is the inevitable outcome of the union. Therefore the reader should automatically infer that, according to my definition, without Love and Justice peace cannot be born.

The role of education in promoting world peace is immeasurable. However, the most effective way to teach peace--and ethics in general--is teaching by example. The great American writer James Baldwin (1924-1987) once said that "Children have never been very good at listening to their elders, but they have never failed to imitate them." Based on this axiom, parents, teachers and all those who fulfill a role model function in society have an enormous responsibility on their shoulders. If they fail to set up the proper example in a manner that is conducive to the promotion of peace, youngsters are surely going to respond accordingly, especially if the role model is the leader of a nation.

On the evening of one of the many tragic shootings in high schools in the United States, the president issued a statement in which he categorically denounced the vicious crime and exhorted the American people to take action against escalating youth violence. He said: "We do know that we must do more to reach out to our children and teach them to express their anger and to resolve their conflicts with words, not weapons."

However, the same news media nationwide that published his comments, abounded with headlines of NATO's unremitting airstrikes on the former Yugoslavia Republic. The United States, being NATO's principal leading member, played a fundamental role in the airstrike campaign. If only the president had learned peace in school and had had good examples to follow, this ambiguity in leadership would have not happened. He would have tried to resolve the conflict with words (diplomacy) not weapons.

The role of education in promoting peace is more crucial than ever before in history. As a renaissance of the Reign of Terror unfolds, violence manifests itself not as a negative aspect of human nature but as an economic, political and sociocultural characteristic of a distraught society. When the 400 richest Americans have about as much wealth as the 50 million households in the bottom half of the population; when a nation has 268 billionaires while 34.5 million people live below the official poverty line; when the top 1 percent of households has more wealth than the entire bottom 95 percent combined, then we know that there is a desperate need to teach peace in our schools according to the principles of Love and Justice--for all.

Apparently, the spreading and growing trend of hate groups in the United States is directly related to this economic disparity. According to a Southern Poverty Law Center Report, an organization that combats hate, intolerance, and discrimination through education and litigation (see resources for details), "a far larger crop of white supremacist youth has sprung from the soil of socioeconomic discontent...They are mainly from one parent or dysfunctional families that are struggling to remain in the lower middle class."

The stifling economic pressure to $ucceed in order to have--not to be--contributes to the despair of a lost generation. When we take into account that the main cause of teenage death is suicide, we immediately know that neither individual nor collective peace prevails in our society, therefore the need to introduce it as a curriculum item in education becomes of paramount importance. The crisis in the educational system stems from this utter disregard to the developmental needs of the human person in contrast to the demands of the economic system. We teach students how to read, write, calculate, memorize data, use technology, while encouraging them to excel academically. Further, we inculcate the fear that without a solid education (technical training, that is), they will not succeed in an increasingly competitive job-market. We extol the efforts of the young scholar but give no kudos to students whose sensitive artistic talents have low--if any-- marketable value. This is economic functionalism of education at its best--or its worst, depending on the vantage point of the observer.

If education is going to fulfill a role in promoting peace, it must begin with a written covenant followed by a plan of action. Actually, the blueprint of this document already exists in the Universal Declaration of Human Rights, proclaimed on December 10, 1948 by the General Assembly of the United Nations; and the Declaration of the Rights of the Child, unanimously adopted by the same international organization on November 20, 1959. Although, these documents are eloquently written, their principles are not duly carried out. Take for example Article 26 of the Universal Declaration of Human Rights, and Principle 10 of the Declaration of the Rights of the Child:

Article 26 (2)
"Education shall be directed to the full development
of the human personality and to the strengthening of
respect of human rights and fundamental freedoms.
It shall promote understanding, tolerance and
friendship among all nations, racial or religious
groups, and shall further the activities of the United
Nations for the maintenance of peace."

Principle 10
"The child shall be protected from practices which
may foster racial, religious and any form of
discrimination. He shall be brought up in a spirit of
understanding, tolerance, friendship among peoples,
peace and universal brotherhood and in full
consciousness that his energy and talents should be
devoted to the service of his fellow men."

Looking at Article 26 (2) of the UN Declaration of
Human Rights, we can clearly notice the discrepancy
between rhetoric and reality. Evidently, education is not
directed to the full development of the human personality-
-much less the development of the human spirit--but
works as a training system that prepares individuals for
the job-market. Neither does the educational system have
a particular program that focuses on promoting
understanding, tolerance and friendship among all
nations. What it does so well is to train students to abide
by norms of conduct, morals and values that are
conducive to the dominant culture, while doing very little
for the maintenance of peace; which should begin,
according to the United Nations itself, with economic
justice.

Similar fallacy is observable in Principle 10 of the
Declaration of the Rights of the Child. As early as pre-
school, children are being robbed of their childhood on
behalf of a premature acquisition of information that will
lead to the development of a functional and productive
worker. In the traditional educational system, there is no
specific curriculum that emphasizes an education in
which a child "shall be brought up in a spirit of
understanding, tolerance, friendship among peoples,
peace and universal brotherhood." Furthermore, the
educational interest of the individual relates to the
potential professional $uccess at the end of the schooling
process, which in the end benefits the economic system at
large. Meanwhile, an education in which individual
talents are developed and devoted to the service of his
fellow-human, is but a blurred vision of a future yet to
come.

In 1795 the German philosopher Immanuel Kant (1724-1804) published a very interesting book entitled *Perpetual Peace*. In this work he stressed that governments must either make collective efforts to ensure survival or face joint self-destruction. More than two hundred years later the issue of peace is more crucial than ever before in human history. Nowadays the wars are no longer limited to armed conflict between nations. Today, industrial-technological societies, under the auspices of economic liberalism, are waging a devastating war against the life-sustaining environment and the dignity of the human being. It is a war fomented by selfishness, greed and unbridled competition in the pursuit of profit.

The race against the clock of survival has already begun. It has become imperative to create an educational plan of action devoted to integral human development. By doing so, education can participate as a front runner in this great race--the human race.

PART III

"The education our situation demanded would enable men to discuss courageously the problems of their context--and to intervene in that context; it would warn men of the dangers of the time and offer them the confidence and the strength to confront those dangers instead of surrendering their sense of self through submission to the decisions of others."

Paulo Freire

"Sed quis custodiet ipsos custodes? (Who will reform the reformers?)

Juvenal
Satires, 6, 1.347

THE REFORM OF EDUCATION

Why is it important to reform education?

Exploring the answer to this question must begin with the distinction between reform of education and education reform. While the former envisions to transform the nature, character, purpose and function of education toward comprehensive human development, the latter merely attempts to restructure the existing educational system in order to generate better academic performance and other pragmatic results. Reforming education invokes substantial individual and social transformation in face of the challenging circumstances of our historical time. Education reform, on the other hand, is based on the economic function needs of the individual, society and the large apparatus that depends on both.

While the proponents of education reform concern themselves with the future of education, we, the reformers of education, dedicate our time, energy and vision to the education of the future. They (bureaucrats) worry about the competitive edge of the workforce and the national economy in an increasingly globalized marketplace. We, educators for human development, embrace the possibility of rehumanizing the individual student in an increasingly mechanized society enslaved by unbridled consumption.

The "education experts" leading this trend are often times enthralled with the role of technology in the future of education. They foresee high-tech schools in cyberspace where learning (acquisition of information) happens continuously at extraordinary speed. In addition, through the corporate owned mass-media, they have managed to influence the public opinion in validating and endorsing the goals of a technology-oriented education for economic functions. Thus, short-sighted and infatuated with the wonders of the electronic world, they fail to observe the colossal challenges of the new millennium, while the human spirit gradually deteriorates.

In the meantime, the reformers of education struggle to enlighten society about the materialistic illusion that links education with the economic system. We know of the desperate and immediate need to implement an education geared toward integral human development (mind, heart and spirit); an education imbued with the principles of (individual) Love and (social) Justice carried out through critical thinking and an open heart. We know it is not only feasible but urgent to deliver an education for human development. Awareness generates responsibility in us to pursue this path of learning, even if the bureaucratic forces hinder our efforts.

The fundamental problem with the education reform movement is not the excessive concern with economic functions or technological advancement; it is the utter neglect to the developmental needs of the student as an evolving human being; the rehumanization process of the individual through education. While technology and science have advanced at astronomical pace in the twentieth century, human development has notoriously deteriorated. The gap drifts farther apart as we struggle to balance a $uccessful economic system with a distraught society of underdeveloped human beings.

Nevertheless, the educational system goes on with the daily task of domesticating and training students to fulfill economic functions. It continuously shoves information into the minds of youngsters claiming it to be knowledge. In fact, Albert Einstein (1879-1955), one of the most brilliant thinkers of all times, acknowledged that it is more important to use your mind to think than to use it as a warehouse for information. This leads to the question of intelligence: is it an energetic resource of the being or a compilation of data in the memory bank? More importantly, however, is to find out what kind of intelligence is one that inflicts self-destruction and does not take action to reverse the process?

The time has come. The fruitless efforts of traditional education reform have proven that what has been attempted does not suit human needs. It serves but the interests of economic functionalism. What human development needs is a reformed educational system in which all the elements of human intelligence are taken into account. It is a new learning paradigm guided in freedom, critical thinking, dialogue and decision making followed by action. This is the backbone of the reform of education movement.

Who and where are the reactionary forces against the reform of education?

The opponents of the reform of education movement are many, authoritarian and everywhere. Ranging from individuals with selfish interests to organizations with a political agenda, these reactionary forces are the main obstacles to integral human development in education. They are powerful, wealthy and have a strong hold on the control of resources, communications and, therefore, are able to manipulate the public opinion. These groups and individuals perceive education as an institution of indoctrination; like the educational system of totalitarian regimes that have been demonized in the past century.

There are numerous organizations that exemplify the indoctrination approach to education bereft of human developmental needs. A quintessential representative of this ilk is the Empower America Education Project. Its mission statement reveals an obsession with an educational system for economic functions and political interests:

> "Empower America is devoted to ensuring that government actions foster growth, economic well-being, freedom and individual responsibility. The ideas that have fueled America's stunning economic expansion--opportunity, competition, ownership and freedom--must be the frame-work of reform of century-old public systems such as K-12 education, the tax code and social security...In implementing our free-market, entrepreneurial principles into law, we are convinced, through actual experience, that we are the most effective "delivery" system in existence...Empower America has demonstrated that is has considerable influence on our core issues-- education reform, technology policy, tax reform, social security reform and national defense."

Why does an organization with such agenda call itself an "education project?" Not once does its mission statement refer to educational objectives related to individual human development, in spite of the fact that the radical conservatives who lead this "education project" are relentless defenders of individual rights. They aim at molding the educational system into conformity with specific ideological, political and economic objectives.

Moreover, when they allude to free-market policies as "the most effective delivery system in existence," it becomes obvious that their primary goal is not education per se, but the promotion of economic and political ideology--like the educational system of totalitarian societies.

Another organization worth mentioning here is Keep the Promise; a partnership of governors, educators and business people. Its purpose is to change the educational system based on the premise that "children must get the education they deserve if our nation is to succeed in a competitive global economy" (clearly what it means is that children must get the utilitarian training that the nation deserves). It is important to emphasize that there is absolutely nothing wrong with an education that benefits national interests; on the contrary, this is a fundamental element of responsible educational practices. However, when these interests are mostly economic in nature and in detriment to the overall educational needs of individual students, then they become objectionable.

Insufficient funding of education is also a major issue of concern, especially for the reform of education that would increase the value of the Humanities and promote individual talents. While billions of dollars are invested in technological and scientific research, education does not receive the same priority, though it yields much higher interests in the national cultural wealth; after all, the quality of a nation is only as good as the quality of its people. Billions more are funneled to the defense budget, which leads the citizen to logically infer that we are constantly preparing for war. Meanwhile, the reform of education movement envisions to promote peace through right human relations among well-developed (opposed to well-trained) individuals.

The military build-up and the scarcity of teachers in the marketplace has engendered an unexpected alliance: the Troops to Teachers Program. This is an initiative for training retiring military personnel to become classroom teachers. The idea is that former military professionals have accumulated experience, are well-trained in giving and receiving directions (orders), and know how to impose discipline. These elements are seen as valuable traits in the traditional educational system. However, having former soldiers as role models for children has the potential to jeopardize the kind of education in which critical thinking, freedom of learning and creative spirit entails. Since a soldier should never question the commands of his superior office, this military culture would inevitably be a part of children's upbringing under the care of a trained military teacher. The positive side is that military personnel are trained to endure hardships and difficult working conditions, which means they would adapt to the teaching profession effortlessly.

Ostensibly, the inception of the military as a teacher source is inspiring many bureaucrats of education. In the state of Louisiana the Governor has proposed a bill requiring students to address teachers and other school employees as "ma'am" or "sir" or at least use the appropriate Mr., Miss, Ms. or Mrs. before the teacher's last name. The bill leaves it up to school boards to decide the punishment of those "disrespectful" students who do not abide by this courtesy title rule. Supposedly, the intent of the bill is to enforce respect (which can only come forth spontaneously otherwise it is coercion not respect); instead, they confuse the students--and themselves--by not distinguishing formality from respect. In the light of the reform of education this misconception of respect is perceived as another unnecessary obstacle between the learner and the educator. Besides, it is up to the teacher, and the teacher alone, to determine how he wants to be called by his students.

These are just a few of numerous and active reactionary forces that strive to postpone the dawn of a new era in education. Because of their specific agenda, they do not benefit from an emerging generation of free-thinking individuals questioning the reality around them. They purposefully discourage any effort for change ignited by questioning. What they promote is a paternalistic education spoon-fed to intellectually, emotionally and spiritually undernourished youngsters. What we, the reformers of education propose, is the liberation of the human spirit from the fetters of economic functionalism in education. We want children to embrace learning as a coveted lifelong endeavor, not a daily drudgery they have to put up with for at least twelve years of their lives. Ultimately, we are committed to the rehumanization process of the individual, society and all its supporting structures.

While their resistance is fueled by a depleting reservoir of archaic educational ideas, our determination is powered by an inexhaustible source of will, cooperation, compassion, love and justice. Considering the nature of the opposing forces, their resistance will timely be gulped up by our determination.

Can the teacher be a social reformer?

From Socrates (c.469-399 BC), who was put to death for encouraging his students to question the inconsistencies of their beliefs, to Jonathan Kozol (1936-   ), who was dismissed from the Boston public school system for questioning its unsuitability and unfair practices, educators have been fulfilling their role as social reformers.

Actually, educators have often been the catalyst for social transformation throughout history. When in 1762 Jean-Jacques Rousseau (1712-1778) published his education treatise *Émile*, he revolutionized the principles of education at the rise of the Age of Enlightenment. His ideas of a child-centered education in which nature and freedom are the main guides to learning, have influenced numerous educators and inspired several educational movements. He strenuously objected to passive learning that made the child a mere obedient automaton of a corrupted society. The central pillar buttressing Rousseau's educational theory is the belief that education not only is important to social reform but is even a prior and necessary condition. Through his writings, Rousseau became the progenitor of one of the most important and dramatic revolutions in human history: The French Revolution.

Another educator/social reformer who enormously influenced educators around the world is Paulo Freire (1921-1997). A champion of freedom and liberation education, he perfected a method for teaching illiterates linking literacy to the development of critical social consciousness. He won international acclaim with the publication of his book *Pedagogy of the Oppressed*, first published in the United States in 1970. Eventually, the book was banned in many totalitarian countries (including Freire's native Brazil) and the writer was compelled to exile in the United States, then in Switzerland and Chile. Nevertheless, Freire's concept of education as an instrument of oppression have not been able to be silenced by those who fearfully object the essence of education as the practice of freedom.

But what is the average classroom teacher to do in order to become a potential instrument for social reform? First and most importantly, she does not indoctrinate, preach or persuade her students to think, believe and act like her or anyone else; regardless of how strongly she thinks and feels about her own truths. What the teacher with a proclivity to be a social reformer does is to encourage his students to question, everything that is imposed upon them, and search for answers through individual critical thinking and group discussions. All that must be presented to the youngster is unbiased facts and data bereft of any ulterior motives. In essence, freedom in education is the first step.

The next phase involves the teacher's commitment to integral human development; a genuine desire to be a participating force in individual and social transformation. With some creativity and imagination, this can be done even within the limiting education parameters set up by the establishment (public or private). Simple acts and words that convey respect, acknowledgement and encouragement can be of utmost value to help youngsters to mature into their own selves. The individual human development ultimately benefits society at large.

Although the critics and originators of quasi-pejorative terms such as "self-esteem education," "social promotion," etc., berate an education with human development concerns, whom of those critics do not need respect, acknowledgement and encouragement in difficult times? If the adult ego gets bruised so easily, what makes education pundits and bureaucrats think that a child or a teenager will handle failure and rejection without further damaging their developmental process?

Reform of education, as in social, economic and political reform, begins with well-educated free thinkers of society. The role of the educator committed to education and social reform is to make sure that the numbers of well-educated free thinkers multiply at geometric proportion. This begins in the classroom with pedagogical activities that promote critical thinking and discussion; like the thirst for knowledge that Socrates summoned his pupils to satiate through questioning. However, nothing can possibly influence youngsters more than the living example set up by their role models. Since the teacher has the potential to be one of the most influential elements in the life of a student, and considering that all knowledge and action begin with the individual, the teacher's participation as a transformational power tool for education and social reform is immeasurable.

A teacher should never doubt her potential and ability to be an effective social reformer. All she has to do is to commit her professional career to human development rather than being a workforce supply clerk. She must look deeper into her mind, heart and spirit and see what her calling to be a teacher truly is; then, act accordingly.

What does the war on drugs have to do with the reform of education?

The use, abuse and the fallacious war on drugs are ubiquitous in every debate regarding social and education reform. The illegal substances are constantly demonized and blamed for many of the social ills afflicting modern society. However, there are many bizarre ambiguities and contradictions in the brouhaha of drug use. While the establishment vehemently condemns the use of drugs, it simultaneously promotes and capitalizes enormous profits from the pharmaceutical industry. The point is what drugs are to be considered legal and socially acceptable and why. This is what the reform of education movement ought to investigate.

It was during the counter-culture revolution of the 1960's that a serious concern with drug use emerged. Until then, drugs were consumed by an insignificant number of two main categories of consumers not posing any particular risk to the *status quo*: artists and intellectuals in one end, the hopeless and dejected in the other. However, the youth of the 1960's popularized the use of drugs as a means of expanding consciousness in a society they viewed as corrupted by economic interests and committed to the barbarities of war in order to secure those interests. To this generation of rebels, drug use became an element of a political agenda for social reform. Consequently, an immediate declaration of war on drugs was but inevitable.

Forty years and billions of dollars later the war on drugs goes on; failing miserably at every step of the way. Prisons are overcrowded with drug users and dealers, consumption has been on the rise for decades, drug lords are more powerful than ever; and worse, there has been substantial evidence of federal agencies involved in the corruption of the illegal business. It is terribly puzzling to fathom why anyone would continuously invest an exorbitant amount of money in an endeavor that is clearly yielding negative results. There must be another reason lurking underneath this policy--and we must ferret it out.

In reality we are society of drug users. We love drugs, and we make an extraordinary profit from the production, advertisement and distribution of these wondrous chemical commodities that consumers gulp up with eager rapacity. Television, radio, internet and all printed media abound with advertisements promoting the consumption of drugs. From alleviating a simple headache to overcoming male impotence, there are a slew of drugs for every (concocted) need.

Often times drugs are introduced in the marketplace without having their potential side effects duly investigated by the Food and Drug Administration. In fact, a report by the Department of Health and Human Services revealed that the FDA learned of 9,961 medication-related deaths and 33,541 hospitalizations in 1997. Nevertheless, the FDA recognized the results of independent studies that estimated that 2 million Americans are hospitalized annually from drug side effects, and 100,000 die each year. And who could ever forget the countless birth defects that approved birth control pills unchained?

Like the lords of the drug cartels, the pharmaceutical companies have one primary goal in mind when launching a new drug on the market: profit. These powerful corporations have research teams both in the laboratories and the marketing department, always sniffing for the lucrative odor in the swamp of illness and pain. Occasionally, they strike gold, as the immensely profitable impotence drug introduced to consumers proved to be. Immediately after this drug became available, the stock value of the pharmaceutical company manufacturing it went skyrocketing, making many investors millionaires overnight. Incidentally, there have been reports of death related to the use of this drug, and the long-term side effects are yet to be seen--it took many years to relate unusual birth defects with the anti-conception drug.

One might argue that the marketing for consumption of drugs in the mass-media is legitimate because those are legal drugs. But what makes a drug legal or illegal? There certainly are many variables that would determine the answer to this question in different societies. For instance, in the Netherlands, sensibility to the problem of drug use in society is a fundamental concern. Since legalizing the so-called soft drugs and regulating hard drugs, that nation has seen some remarkable positive results, ranging from a decline in crime rates to substantial reduction of drug use. Seemingly, they have overcome the problem by making peace with drugs, rather than waging an expensive and fruitless war on drugs.

Meanwhile, we continue to use the same archaic and unproductive tactics attempting to curb drug use in the United States. And yet, from early childhood to the senior years, Americans are consuming an extraordinary amount of drugs--legal and illegal. There are children, as young as one-year-old, who cannot function properly without drugs. Teenagers with weight control problem gulp up appetite suppressants to maintain a positive self-esteem. And high caliber $uccessful executives would succumb to utter depression if it weren't for mood enhancing drugs widely available on the market. Add to this the unverifiable number of consumers of illegal drugs and what we have is a nation of addicts selling a hypocritical message to youngsters to say no to drugs.

However, the most pathetic contradiction and ambiguity of the problem of drugs in our society is the high and unrestrained consumption of alcoholic beverages. Alcohol is not only legal but readily available in every city corner. It kills more people in the United States than all the other drugs combined. There even is a prominent organization of mothers who have lost their children, directly or indirectly, to individuals under the influence of this inebriating drug; perhaps the most popular drug among adolescents and young adults. Many hundreds of thousands of people have suffered serious health problems caused by the abuse of this socially acceptable drug. Thus, considering this dismal scenario, why then is it legal, or at least not strictly regulated? The massive media advertisement of this product can hint you into one of the many possible answers: profit.

Similar issue came about in recent years regarding the highly addictive and health damaging consequences of yet another legal drug: cigarette smoking. Individuals, families and even states have filed law suits against cigarette manufacturers. In what would have been hilarious if it were not tragic, during the initial trials some of these companies claimed innocence to the charges. They backed their arguments on studies conducted by scholars whose research evinced that cigarette smoking was not addictive; research funded by the tobacco industry itself.

The drug problem afflicting our society is real and deserves critical examination. It affects children, young adults and older citizens alike. The central issue, however, is not to run an advertisement campaign to discourage drug use but to investigate what are the roots of the problem in the first place. Boredom, discontentment, hopelessness are among some of the many symptoms attributed to this social plague, though they are not themselves the cause. Regardless of the causes or circumstances one simple truth stands on solid evidence: the costly war on drugs has done absolutely nothing to ameliorate the situation; on the contrary, it has aggravated it considerably and in manifold ways.

The reform of education movement must tackle this problem with open mind, heart and spirit. Now that even teachers are being required to undertake drug tests in order to get a public school teaching job in certain states--a blatant violation of the Fourth Amendment of their constitutional rights--the time has come to face the issue of drug use in our society as any other legal addiction (sex, gambling, working, etc.), and not as a biased taboo deeply ingrained in retrograde policies based on prejudice and fear.

The reformers of education should not openly advocate either legalization or prohibition of drug use, for that would contradict their commitment to freedom and critical thinking in education. Their responsibility, what they must do, is to question the current policies and the alternatives available. The questioning should trailblaze its way to an appropriate answer.

Do we need to rehumanize the individual in order to reform education?

Actually, the opposite takes place. We need to reform education in order to rehumanize the individual, for it is with education that individual and social transformation begins.

A reform of education committed to integral human development envisions to reverse current dehumanizing conditions. This is based on the education philosophy of Social Reconstructionism; a ramification of the Progressive education movement concerned with social change. Social Reconstructionist educators view Progressive education as the vehicle, not only for social and educational reform but to the creation of a new society. Ultimately, they embrace the postulate that humankind is in a state of profound cultural and ethical crisis. They utilize the social sciences of economics, anthropology, sociology, political science and psychology as the working tools with which to build a truly humane education and social order.

In addition to awakening students' consciousness about social problems--and encouraging them to search for a solution; to take action!--Social Reconstructionists believe that a just and equitable social order can only come about when conscientious educators challenge obsolete conceptions of knowledge associated with the dominant educational system. Within this educational strategy, the teacher's primary professional objective is to foster the advent of a new kind of citizen; one that utilizes the instruments of science and technology on behalf of human welfare instead of the sheer pursuit of profit. Moreover, these educators of a renaissance era of learning are to encourage critical thinking in freedom, using group discussions to solve problems and improve social welfare of all citizens.

Social Reconstructionism, as mentioned above, is a ramification of the Progressive movement, which stresses that all learning should focus on the child's interests and needs, rather than on the needs of schooling as a training program of the workforce. Considering that rehumanization is both an interest and need of the young human, it ought to be a fundamental aspect of the educational process. However, reactionary forces in service of an educational system dominated by economic functionalism purposefully hinder the expansion of human consciousness. After all, a rehumanized group of individuals whose values are solidly based on solidarity, cooperation and mutual concern with the well-being of the entire social organism, would be extremely detrimental to the selfish, competitive and egoistic profit seeking interests of a few.

When observing the trends of educational (under)development in relation to sociological statistics and information (hate crime, wanton violence, poverty, etc.), it becomes crystal clear that the current educational system is rooted in a terribly misleading dichotomy. On one hand, it promotes the elementary knowledge necessary for the student to fulfill her economic function in society, while simultaneously neglecting her most fundamental needs for human development. And if we take into consideration the pressing challenges of our times, this myopic educational vision of training citizens for the economic system, in lieu of a holistic education, is likely to lead to the blindness of the human spirit.

Both intelligence and knowledge can also be ambiguous in their nature. While the latter is the outcome of the former, often they are completely dissociated from all the other elements that integrate into the complexity of human intelligence. Indifference to the general welfare of humanity is a typical expression of egotistical intelligence, which is supported by a branch of knowledge (intellectual) severed from the trunk of wisdom, whose roots go deep into emotional and spiritual learning.

Ostensibly, rehumanizing education is the imperative first step toward integral human development. In this new education paradigm, what really counts is not what the student knows but who he is to himself and in relation to society. Furthermore, the awareness that humanity must be the center and purpose of all technological and economic development becomes an indisputable characteristic of educational practices, otherwise modernization can be a potential danger to social order. It is important to notice that while development is modernization, not all modernization is development.

Since the understanding of being truly human has faded in the bedazzlement with technological and economic development, rehumanizing the educational system is the first step toward integral human development.

Is the reform of education a pre-condition for social reform?

Absolutely!

The hullabaloo to renew the educational system is subtly related to the unspoken demand for social reform, though the powers-that-be manage to convince the public opinion that it all relates to academic performance.

One of the most relevant problems of modern times is the question of education; what it is, how it should be and for what purpose. This issue affects every single component of individual and social development. Unfortunately, contemporary mainstream education is utterly alienated from the most essential aspects of life. In fact, it does not even serve the needs of the economic-political system it is supposed to entertain, as the so-called educational crisis evinces. Therefore, it is becoming momentous for education to undergo a dramatic metamorphosis of purpose, while re-evaluating the concepts of knowledge, intelligence and the nature of learning.

As far as the connection between education and social reform is concerned, Rudolf Steiner (1861-1925), the founder of Waldorf Education, emphasizes the historical demand of a "threefold social organism:" socialism in economics, democracy in justice, and freedom in cultural life. He stresses that the need to reform education is tantamount to the need for liberty in cultural life, equality in the democratic state, and brotherly love in associative economic life. In fact, as an educator and social reformer, Steiner unified his political and social reform vision with the creation of a truly human education. He exemplified the fact that teachers must have a voice in how society is reformed.

In this age of globalization, education has to face up the duty of midwifing the birth of a world society painfully struggling to be born. This is in itself a social reform that calls for a concomitant reform of education. However, the emphasis on social change must go far beyond economic relations and internationalization of free-market economy. Both reforms, educational and social, demand a reevaluation of economic justice and social democracy in a globalized world community of rehumanized individuals.

Knowledge or wisdom?

According to most dictionaries, the difference between knowledge and wisdom is simply a matter of subtle semantics. However, each has its own specific meaning and value; in definition as well as in pragmatic use.

As mentioned in Part II, The Merriam Webster's Collegiate Dictionary, Tenth Edition, defines knowledge as "the fact or condition of knowing something, the fact or condition of having information or being learned." The same dictionary defines wisdom as "accumulated philosophic or scientific learning." The latter definition is not only more vague than the former but infinitely more disturbing, for it relates wisdom to the Cartesian concept of rational knowledge (philosophy and science). Like the modern--and yet obsolete--educational system, it leaves out essential components that constitute the human complexity, such as the emotional and spiritual aspects of human nature.

Wisdom is to reform of education what knowledge is to education reform. One envisions a radical restructuring of the educational foundation by incorporating emotional and spiritual development, while the other remains narrowly focused on re-adapting an already proven failed system that basically stresses accumulation of information. In the reform of education movement the objective is "to be" knowledge (the Cartesian axiom would change to "I am knowledge, therefore I know"). In education reform for economic function the mode is based on "to have" knowledge (the Cartesian axiom then is "I have knowledge, therefore I think I know").

While wisdom is the pinnacle of knowing on all levels of human intelligence, knowledge, if associated to the intellect alone, can have strong ties with ignorance. For instance, an imbalanced individual with an extraordinary amount of knowledge can display significant signs of ignorance, as the case of the Unabomber referred to earlier exemplifies. Perhaps this is what the book of Genesis relates to when it says "you must not eat from the tree of knowledge of good and evil;" or what Francis Bacon (1561-1626) averred: "Knowledge without love can be profoundly corrupt and evil." Furthermore, was the invention of nuclear weapons a result of intelligence or haughty ignorance triggered by competitive struggle? Did it come about as a genuine effect of intellectual activity or as an outcome of fear, oppression and dissension? Thus, a knowledge that happens exclusively in the intellectual domain lacks the wisdom our critical historical time demands.

Taking Francis Bacon's postulate for granted, the reform of education movement must investigate the possibility of combining knowledge with love. Since the love of knowledge already exists in our society (we can also attribute this trend to Bacon who asseverated that "knowledge is power"), what is sorely needed nowadays is the knowledge of love.

Is Love a mode of knowledge?

Philippus Aureolus Paracelsus (1493-1541), a Swiss alchemist and physician, asserted that "He who knows nothing, loves nothing. But he who understands also loves, notices, sees...The more knowledge is inherent in a thing, the greater the love."

Inferentially, at least according to him, love is not only a mode of knowledge but an intrinsic element of it. Love, however, does not originate in the intellect but in the emotional body, though people often apply the Cartesian mode of love in their lives (I think I love, therefore I do). The fact is we can only love what we know; and, as a general rule, people we love the most are those we know best. Moreover, it is utterly impossible to love with the mind, as much as it is impossible to rationalize with the heart. But what does all of this have to do with reform of education? Everything.

First of all, let's make it clear, we are not talking about romantic love here. As a mode of knowledge, therefore a matter of educational concern, the love we want to investigate as a learning discipline is what the Greeks called Agape; which is referred to in religious literature as both God's love for humanity and people for one another. It is the element that might have been concealing the answer to the problems of human existence--and the unfettered violence in world history.

Many scholars, intellectuals and artists have studied, proposed and displayed the means by which this neglected mode of knowledge can be incorporated in education. Leo Buscaglia (1924-1998), Erich Fromm (1900-1980) and Albert Schweitzer (1875-1965) are but a few of many prominent sensitive thinkers who have left a wealth of information on the art and knowledge of loving. Unfortunately, their legacy has not been duly utilized by an educational system primarily focused on intellectual development and preparation for economic functions. Another not so obvious reason is the subtle threat that love poses to the dominant economic system, for the principles underlying the free-market approach are incompatible with the principles of love. One preaches competition while the other emphasizes cooperation; one stresses selfishness and greed, the other nurtures itself on community and simplicity. Borrowing Erich Fromm's terminology, one is necrophilic (fascination with death) the other is biophilic (fascination with life).

Despite the desperately imminent need to equip children with knowledge of love, the bureaucrats of education, their lackeys in the business world and even some religious leaders remain oblivious to the task. They orchestrate all sorts of superficial and inane initiatives to curb the escalating problem of violence in our society. As I write, legislation is pending in ten states that would either require or permit the Ten Commandments to be posted in public schools. The naive (or cunning proselytizers) supporters of this bill claim such a move would help stem school violence. I can only surmise they also believe that posting important chapters of Criminal Law in the inner city streets would also peter out crime. Incidentally, I suggest law makers posting a copy of the Bill of Rights (with the first amendment highlighted) on the door of their offices to remind them of the Constitution they must serve.

Perhaps, the bureaucrats and politicians have good intentions in their callow actions; maybe. What they certainly do not have is the knowledge of love within themselves, otherwise they would know it cannot be inculcated. They would also know that violence and hatred are, basically, manifestations of lack of love not of religious morality. Love is something that if they know at all, is but an intellectual conception of what should be experienced in the heart.

Love as a mode of knowledge cannot exist as a duty. It is impossible to coerce a child to love his parents, siblings, friends, fellow-citizens or country. Those who wish to be loved must behave so as to elicit love, but it is utterly hopeless to expect genuine love by coercion. What remains to be seen is if love can be learned.

Is it possible to teach students how to love?

Psychologists, psychiatrists, sociologists, anthropologists and educators have suggested in several studies and research that love can be a learned discipline-- a learned response, a learned emotion. Hence, it ought to be a teachable subject.

Moved by the suicide of a brilliant young female student of his, Leo Buscaglia decided he should do something about human development education that was absent in academia. Thus, he created and introduced what turned out to be a very popular course entitled Love at the University of Southern California. Eventually, it became an equally popular book of the same title. However, would it be possible to create a similar successful program at the elementary, middle, and secondary level of education? Why not?

When considering the possibility of teaching love, at any level, two interdependent premises must be observed: you cannot teach what you do not know, and you cannot know what you do not study and practice. Since most teachers, if any at all, never learned about the art of loving as a learning discipline--much less teaching it as such--they must first understand what it means to themselves and the educational process of their students. Remember, we are not referring to any specific form of love, but general characteristics intrinsic in the nature of love itself--care, concern, consideration, solidarity, compassion, cooperation, etc.

In order to attempt teaching love as a curriculum discipline, it is imperative to be fully aware that love cannot be inculcated into anyone. It is a genuine act of freedom. In addition, it requires elementary knowledge of human nature, historical patterns (as an analytical tool), commitment and plenty of practice in interpersonal and social relationships. The challenge is how to carry out such an audacious program in an educational system dominated by intellectual and technical knowledge. Firstly, we must reform education if we ever want to see such initiative instituted as a fundamental educational component. Secondly, there must be a revival of the Humanities in education; not as a mechanism for cultural refinement only, but as an instrument for emotional awareness and individual transformation.

Considering the dismal circumstances of the educational system today, the appalling violence assailing our schools and society, and the gargantuan problems of the modern world, implementing a curriculum program to teach how to love is, as Fromm averted, "the only sane and satisfactory answer to the problem of human existence." It is feasible, necessary and urgent.

The time has come in which the love of learning is learning to love.

To reform or not to reform: is there a question?

After everything discussed hitherto, is there still any question left regarding the imminent need to reform education? It depends on the mind-frame of the reader. If he thinks the role, purpose and future of education is to contribute to producing a qualified workforce, to develop technology and science, and to expand, unremittingly, the economic system--with all its costs and consequences--then, improving academic performance and pseudo-civic skills are to remain the precarious foundation of the educational system. On the other hand, if she believes that education must serve human development (individual/social), instead of the interests of a self-seeking economic system; if she believes we have reached the crucial turning point in human history in which the concomitant education of mind, heart and spirit is of paramount importance to the welfare of humanity and the life-sustaining environment we depend on, then, reforming education is not a question but a responsibility and a duty that must be acted upon--immediately!

In order to take action, we must become aware that education is a powerful social force that has been misused--and abused--by special interests groups (business, government, religion, etc.) throughout history: Ancient Greece and its training of citizens; the monopoly of knowledge during the Scholasticism period; the Soviet Union indoctrination system; and the Western world propaganda of righteousness, have all utilized education as a self-serving manipulation tool. Meanwhile, genuine human development has been neglected, and the signs, like festering wounds, are open for everyone to see. Consequently, at the apex of intellectual development, humanity stands on the edge of the abyss of self-destruction, where technology and economic prosperity co-exist with deadly serious environmental crisis, hatred, violence and appalling indifference to human suffering.

Nevertheless, the educational system follows its masters like an obedient puppy. It does not dare to bring awareness of the critical challenges youngsters--to whom the future belongs--will confront as they grow up, for critical consciousness is detrimental to selfish special interests. Thus, the brouhaha about the crisis in education is an oxymoronic attempt to improve an educational system that will worsen the situation. More intellectual knowledge, more skills, more economic functionalism, while widening the gap between the highly sophisticated intellectual individual and the emotionally/spiritually underdeveloped human being. I call this *Educacide*, that is, the murder of education.

As Paulo Freire wisely observed, "as the oppressors dehumanize others and violate their rights, they themselves also become dehumanized." Therefore it is only the oppressed who, by freeing themselves, can free their oppressors. In similar context, education, as an oppressed entity, must liberate itself from the oppressing bureaucratic system. Since teachers are the main pillars supporting this most valuable social institution, the responsibility for liberation lies primarily on their shoulders. They owe it to their students, their community, their nation, the world and to themselves.

To reform or not to reform? That's no longer a question. The only remaining issue is how teachers can trigger the process by themselves. But before establishing a plan of action teachers must first unite.

PART IV

"It is not possible to discuss the situation further unless we recognize the social organism in its three aspects: socialism in economic life, democracy in the life of rights, and freedom or individuality in cultural life. That is, in truth, the only salvation for humanity."

Rudolf Steiner

"The great aim of education is not knowledge but action."

Herbert Spencer

TEACHERS OF THE WORLD, UNITE!

Preamble to Part IV

The questions in the past three segments of this book have led to a critical bifurcation: teachers either explore the possibilities for conscientious action for change or despondency takes over. Since educators are inherently meant to be warriors of knowledge and guardian angels of the youth, giving up the battle in despair is not even a remote possibility. Therefore what remains ahead is the pathway toward the reform of education, whose main activists (teachers) are the catalysts for positive change.

Hence, remaining true to the Socratic approach of questioning, this section investigates a few possibilities for transformative action through a series of "how to" questions that might usher a new era in education. The struggle will continue on until the envisioned transformation has become a reality; until integral human development in freedom has become an inviolable individual and social right.

A final caveat: brilliant ideas and passionate aspirations, if not acted upon, are as useless as moronic thinking and an empty heart.

How to inspire hope in education and teachers?

According to Dante Alighieri (1265-1321), the author of the *Divine Comedy*, the motto on the gates of hell reads: "Abandon hope, all you who enter here." Since education has not marched through the threshold of inferno yet, hope is the propelling energy of its transformation.

Indeed, hope is the positive expectation that there is a way out; a solution for life's most pressing challenges. Without it, problems are death sentences and answers are not born. It is a decisive element in any attempt to bring about improvement of circumstances. However, hope is not meant to be passive (as the Spanish word esperar, which at the same time means waiting and hoping), but a positive attitude in which intellectual and emotional forces act on generating results. In other words, hope means action.

However, the hullabaloo about the educational crisis publicized every day in the media, creates an atmosphere of subtle hopelessness in society. Seldom, if ever, does a headline convey good news about education in general or teachers in particular; which is understandable since sensationalistic bad news is what fosters competition in the mass-media. Consequently, people become skeptical, uninterested and discouraged to do anything that could reverse the dreary trends of the modern educational system. Instead, they surrender their hope to the bureaucrats who manipulate the situation according to their own special interests. Thus, it is up to teachers to take charge and show society that the teaching class can offer an alternative. Teachers must convey to the public that they are the incarnation of hope itself.

In order to convince anyone of anything, we must first believe in it ourselves. Teachers cannot pretend to exude hope if, in reality, they feel utterly hopeless. But how can a professional group that is unappreciated, overworked and underpaid exude hope to the society it toils for? The first step is to build a support group coalition for mutual appreciation and encouragement; a network of like-minded individuals committed to improving themselves as stewards of education for the development of humanity. This will gradually strengthen the self-esteem of the teaching class, while reinforcing the ties with one another and the community. The seeds of hope have just been planted.

For more effective results, teachers should organize locally at the grassroots level in every school district in the nation. Through newsletters, Web sites, among other creative means of communication, the micro organizations would connect nationally in order to empower each small unit of the whole. This initiative would give birth to an unprecedented professional culture in which all teachers can relate, integrate, participate--and act! The seeds of a plan of action have just been planted.

It is important to stress that this grassroots movement must be completely independent from the unions and associations. As discussed earlier in this book, unions, although essential professional organizations, often times take conservative stands that do not necessarily reflect the best interest of education for human development. Moreover, they are primarily geared toward specific professional interests such as labor disputes, working conditions, etc. However, the grassroots movement envisioned here, is aimed at bringing teachers together as a brotherhood/sisterhood of public servants committed to transforming, not only education but a dismal social reality. We shall protest and withstand excessive selfishness, greed, prejudice, violence, hatred, and, ultimately, hopelessness. In addition, it intends, after coalescing the fraternity of teachers, to establish a social affiliation with the community at large, to which exclusively professional organizations such as unions would not relate.

Another important aspect to emphasize in the effort to promote hope is the proliferation of good news. If left to the mass-media, the news stories will either report what is not working or deprecate teachers and education altogether--occasionally it also works as a forum for politicians, bureaucrats and pseudo-pundits. Seldom are uplifting articles published; and when they are, they do not take the same overtone of sensationalistic commercial (debased) news. Therefore it is the responsibility of teachers to divulge all relevant news that promotes the good work and deeds of individual teachers and the class at large. Ultimately, it is our responsibility to disseminate teachers' positive image.

Here is an example of a missed opportunity. The New York Times News Service recently ran a piece of unprecedented human value involving a teacher. Jane Smith, a 42-year-old middle school teacher in North Carolina, was constantly telling her student Michael Carter to pull up his baggy pants, until she found out he couldn't because he was on dialysis and needed a kidney transplant. After more than a year Michael tried, unsuccessfully, to find a matchable donor, Smith, who has a 12-year-old son herself, underwent a battery of tests and found out she was a suitable match to Michael. Without hesitating, she volunteered to undergo surgery in order to donate one of her kidneys to her ailing student. If saving the life of her student through self-sacrifice were not alone a phenomenal act of love and bravery, the fact that Smith is white and Michael is an African American boy is a powerful social statement in our racially divided society. Teacher Jane Smith is the incarnation of hope in an extremely selfish-oriented and racially divided society.

Despite the extraordinary devotion and uniqueness of her action, Jane Smith, the teacher who sacrificed herself for her diseased student, remains unknown to most of her colleagues and the members of the society to which she belongs. To the best of my knowledge there has been no major recognition; and I do not mean an award, a letter of acknowledgement or any other superficial expression of gratitude, but something tantamount to her exemplary unselfish act. In a culture in which greed and selfishness are cherished values, Jane Smith is a unique individual and teacher. She should and deserves to be professionally, monetarily and socially rewarded. Standing in front of a classroom full of children, she is a superb role model for human development and social transformation.

Meanwhile, the average teacher around the country wonders about his individual role in the pursuit of positive change. Even if courageous and hopeful, she may feel alienated from the decision making process of education reform, therefore impotent to make a difference. This is one of the reasons a coalition of grassroots support groups can be a source of encouragement. Notwithstanding, it would behoove every teacher to know that he alone stands at his own center of transformative power. Each one of us can-- and must--make a difference.

How to make a difference on your own?

Many people disregard the power of one. They think of themselves as insignificant isolated members of a society in which anonymous relations prevail. This is particularly true in metropolitan areas and aggravated by electronic means of communication. Moreover, participation in social processes is so abstract and mass-oriented, people tend to disbelieve they can make a difference as independent individuals--the extremely low turnaround at election booths endorses this claim.

In reality, everything done in society is done by individuals. Numerous are the men and women who have single-handedly made an indelible mark in the world. The problem is that, in order to conform, many people surrender their individualities to the dominant culture, the taboos, the pseudo-morality, the information and misinformation spoon-fed to them. Consequently, they end up believing that the individual is less important than the group of which he is a member. They become untrue to the highest aspirations and convictions of their beings, while allowing themselves to be governed by the customs and conventions of the group. Essentially, it is a matter of integrity. Thus, if you really want to be a power in the world, you must be your genuine self.

To the teacher, self-asserting herself can be particularly daunting, especially if she holds controversial opinions. At a time when teachers are being severely criticized for "not delivering academic performance," it is extremely difficult--and dangerous-- to express point of views contradictory to those of the *status quo*. Hence, she might feel inclined to succumb to the external pressures in order to keep her livelihood and pay her bills. Here is when unions and grassroots support groups can be invaluable professional assets. Nevertheless, it is possible for a teacher to be a unique professional whose work makes a positive difference in education, even while remaining cautious of the dictatorial bureaucracy. There are many ways to carry out the task. Let's examine a few of the possibilities, beginning where it counts the most: the classroom.

It all begins in the classroom. It is the stage where the teacher performs his act, art and craft. His audience is composed of youngsters who, in most cases, did not come to the show out of their own volition. They sit there because it is a mandatory requirement imposed upon them by parents and society. If the show does not captivate them, they are likely to develop a lifelong distaste for the wondrous art of learning. It is a weighty responsibility on the teacher's shoulders.

In order to ensure the success of the production, the teacher, like an artist, must keep the interest of her audience at all times. This can be a truly challenging task for the teacher, considering the stale, rote memory, textbook- oriented learning advocated in schools. However, with creativity, artistic expression in teaching, and freedom--the latter must be surreptitiously snatched--it is possible to create a pleasant learning environment for both the teacher and her students. If she succeeds in transforming daily drudgery into regular excitement, she will be able to cultivate critical thinking, emotional and spiritual development (in freedom through the Humanities, not proselytizing), thereby exerting an extraordinary influence in her pupils' lives.

However, nothing the teacher does can be more powerful in influencing his students than his own being. It is not what he knows but who he is that influences the child most deeply. His words may convince students of the right or wrong of an issue, but his personality, behavior and actions will draw them to the teacher's realm of influence like metal to a magnet. Children instinctively seek in their teacher a model for their own development. Although there is a sense of risk in this possibility, considering a professional whose ethics

70

might be questionable, for the teacher with a genuine commitment to education in freedom, this is a reward for his ontological vocation. It is his opportunity to contribute to the human development of society through the production of quality individuals.

In order to bring forth human excellence, teachers must be of quality themselves. They should diligently work on self-improvement that goes beyond the narrowly limited scope of professional development, if they truly intend to affect young lives by being living examples. In addition, they should make a conscientious effort to participate, individually and collectively, in the transformational process of education for human development. There is a remarkable organization called Triangles in Education (see resources for more information) that seek to promote Soul-oriented education for all peoples. It works in a way in which individual participation occurs in connection with two other educators, forming a triangle of energy through the power of will. It is a marvelously effective strategy utilizing faith in a non-sectarian manner.

Another monumental way to make a difference on your own is to communicate; openly, in writing, speaking and listening (yes, listening is a form of communication). Whenever an educational issue stimulates your senses, get active and express yourself loudly and clearly. Write letters to the editor of your local newspaper on a regular basis, write articles to magazines, newsletters and other publications covering educational topics; or even better, create your own newsletter and make it widely available. Speak to students and parents about sensitive issues concerning educators--they do not have a slight idea of what teachers have to endure--organize presentations in your local library and speak to community members. And most importantly, listen to everyone who has concerns, suggestions, praises or criticisms about education. Whatever you decide to do, be creative in your approach and remain actively involved. Your individual contribution is invaluable, indeed.

While on the topic of communication, do not forget to voice your opinion to lawmakers. Some of them have been building political careers on ill-advised policies that deeply affect the teaching class. Let them know you and I are ready to fight back. All we need is to get public opinion support. In the end, the bureaucracy is but a paper tiger; literally.

How to confront the bureaucracy?

It seems like every day there is an assault on education and teachers in the media. The subject has become so (un)popular that it has been deftly exploited in political campaigns. In recent years, lawmakers have touted new bills aimed at, so they claim, holding educators more accountable for their job performance. Actually, teachers' job performance is gauged by students' academic performance measured by standardized test results. Furthermore, new legislation have eliminated tenure, limited teacher pay and weakened teachers' collective bargaining rights, among other travesties of an educational system running amok in the hands of those who do not belong in the field. The time has come to claim it back.

Education and teachers have become the scapegoats for a plethora of social problems that reflect themselves in the school system. Alcohol abuse, drug use, rape, suicide, etc., are but a few social dysfunctions not yet gauged by a national standardized test. However, the most prominent one is the barbaric violence taking place in the school grounds--as I write, the news media reports that a six year old first-grade boy has shot dead a girl classmate in school. Incidentally, juvenile crime and detention have more than doubled in the last fifteen years. Most of those young offenders are afflicted by poverty and mental illness; two widespread features in these times of economic prosperity.   Nevertheless, the vote-seeking politicians and their business supporters focus their myopic vision of education on academic performance, since this is where their immediate and selfish interests lie. The long-term investment in human development has become a superfluous item on their educational agenda.

Inferentially, teachers must reclaim the decision-making power of education by virtue of merit and rights. It is interesting to observe that the teacher must be licensed and adequately trained in order to exercise the duties of teaching. However, no requirements are imposed on those who make critical decisions on educational policies. Several school superintendents in this country have absolutely no educational background--not to mention the lawmakers. It is with the teaching class that the power of education must be.

However, because education is intrinsically connected with various segments of social life, teachers do need public support to carry out the colossal responsibility of preparing future generations. They must apply the same propaganda tactics utilized by the bureaucrats to wheedle public opinion, though in this case they have legitimate arguments and interests.

They, the mongers of utilitarian education, appeal to collective subconscious fears (of parents in particular) that without amassing information galore, students will not succeed in an increasingly competitive job-market. Meanwhile, we, the proponents of human development in freedom, must beseech members of society (parents being the most critical allies) to realize that preparation for an economic function, though an important element of schooling, should not sacrifice the general welfare, happiness and innermost aspirations of children. There is much we can do.

Every day the national media reports on various data that, directly or indirectly, relates to education and human development. Articles on teenage suicide (the United States, by the way, has the highest teen suicide rate in the world), legal drug abuse (millions of children are medicated daily so they can learn how to behave and cope), youth violence, hate crime and a smorgasbord of social tragedies involving youngsters are daily features in the national panorama. You can utilize this downhearted information to elucidate the public opinion, especially parents, that the serious problems of education are not poor academic performance but deterioration of human development. By clipping and photocopying articles (make sure it falls under the fair use policy), accompanied by a written commentary of your own, you can distribute these through different venues--even mail them to lawmakers. This will catapult an educational awareness program. Can you imagine the social impact if every teacher in the nation begins campaigning in this way? Notes to parents, letters to the editors, articles, newsletters, flyers, every day, everywhere, by every teacher in the country? That is the power of freedom. Let's use it.

The commercialization of education is another problem that must be addressed. Aware of youngsters consumption potential, corporations have invaded and taken over schools more aggressively than the Third Reich's invasion of Poland. The difference, however, is that the world vehemently condemned the latter and World War II broke out; but the former has been, with the exception of some defiant organizations, passively accepted.

Throughout the United States, schools are distastefully decorated with advertisements of brand-name products. Soft drink companies have been brokering deals with school districts for the exclusive rights to sell their unhealthy products to kids, while cajoling lifetime customers. However, nothing could be more deplorable than applying curriculum programs for marketing products under the guise of education. There are books that teach math to children by counting specific candy brand-name. Classroom business courses that teaches students the value of work by showing them how famous fast-food restaurants are run. Worse yet, there is a broadcast system in the classroom enforcing it all.

Channel One Network, a commercial-filled television news program that is broadcast into 40% of secondary schools nationwide, is a typical example of how private interests are turning the public school system into a for-profit business. Every day millions of students (8 million students in 12,000 schools to be precise) begin their day with current events and commercials transmitted by Channel One. Its producer loans television sets and video equipment to schools that guarantee students will watch the consumer training program during class time. Similarly, a Silicon Valley-based company called ZapMe, offers schools thousands of dollars worth of computer equipment loaded with advertisements targeting students as potential customers. These companies are well-aware that, according to American Demographics, children 4 to 12 spent an estimated $24.4 billion in 1997 alone. To them, it is a matter of expanding business. To us, it is matter of principles. Schools are social institutions of learning--in freedom--not an open market for the proliferation of economic policies.

The Center for Commercial-Free Public Education (see resources for information) is a non-profit organization that addresses the issue of commercialism in our public schools. Every citizen concerned with the prostitution of the educational system, should contact this organization and get involved in the struggle against the corporate take-over of our schools--the next step after having taken over our government. The Center for Commercial-Free Public Education sponsors several programs to combat this commercial travesty. Among them are: CAP (Community Assistance Program), which supports community organizers with materials, local coalition building and assistance for teachers, students, parents, school board members and others. School Watch Team is a national volunteer watchdog group that reports current and planned advertising schemes in schools. Unplug, a youth organizing program, helps students oppose commercialism in their schools. And Classroom Pledge Campaign, a national pledge campaign for individuals, classes and organizations.

Unfortunately, many teachers seem oblivious to the damage such manipulation of our schools and students represents. In fact, the president of the Colorado Springs Education Association, a predominantly conservative region, stated that "We haven't had a single complaint" against corporate-sponsored programs. In the same area, a middle school science teacher was reported to have said: "You just don't turn down a deal that will bring $20,000 a year to your school." Is money the yardstick with which to measure what we should allow in our schools? What a meretricious attitude!

It would also behoove us to be aware of companies like Advantage Schools, Inc., that seek to make money by running public charter schools. They carefully select their principals, giving preference for those who have business experience or a M.B.A. degree. Their philosophy is clearly evinced in the words of a head of one of their schools who said: "Children are our products, if we don't produce quality products, parents will take their business elsewhere." This is the epitome of the economic functionalism of education, and an educational tragedy as far as human development is concerned. Comparing the education of a child to producing a product is pathetic. This is more than the corporate presence in our schools; this is the school as a corporation itself. Scrupulous educators, and those who genuinely care for education for human development, must create an alliance; a coalition against the commercialization of schools and students.

The signs of rebellion are gradually appearing on the educational scene. Some courageous students are already taking action and are determined to ignite a movement for the reform of education on their own terms. Take for example the actions of Bill Wetzel, the founder and director of *Power to the Youth*, a primarily Web-based organization aimed at encouraging young people to take charge of their schools. The Web site (www.youthpower.net) explains the purpose of the organization, offers suggestions to take action, and even has an inspiring selection of quotes by famous personalities such as Albert Einstein ("It's a miracle that curiosity survived formal education) and Mark Twain ("I have never let my schooling interfere with my education"),among many others.

Wetzel is a young man with a vision and the determination to make a difference in the world. He is prodding the awareness of other youngsters who are blindly following an educational process that makes them miserable, daily. In the Power to the Youth Web site he proclaims: "We must demand freedom--the freedom to pursue our own interests and live our lives as we choose...Do you wish there was something you could do? Well, there is! We need to get involved...The world is crying out for our help. Plain and simple, this place is getting ugly and we are going to do something about it."

If individual teachers and organizations were to join forces with conscientious students like Bill Wetzel, a new paradigm of education could surface. Furthermore, if parents became educated and aware of the threats to the individuality and happiness of their children, they would certainly join the coalition and the dictatorial authority of the bureaucracy would be substantially diminished--if not eliminated.

You may say I am a dreamer, but as long as I am not the only one, we may all wake up to an unprecedented educational system in which individual human development determines what is right, good and necessary.

In the meantime, teachers and students should organize at the grassroots level, and gradually involve parents in the proliferation of the new educational culture. Parents are the most crucial allies in the movement, and they must be made aware of how counterfeit education has become and how it affects the well-being of their beloved children. In addition, alternative education schools, associations and organizations, which are already carrying out the reform of education in their own terms, can and should be drafted into the national coalition for reform of education for human development in freedom.

As numerous organizations have proven, the World Wide Web is an extraordinary vehicle to establish, connect, promote and even act toward education and social reform.

How to utilize technology to strengthen the movement?

The world has become a cyberworld. A growing number of people of all age groups and backgrounds have access to the Internet. Although it is tragic that many are getting addicted to this new electronic drug--a study revealed that almost 6 percent; that is, more than 11 million Internet users suffer from some form of addiction--we cannot ignore the potential to reach out and network with people all over the world.

Without getting into the cyber sewer (misuse, commercialization, pedophilia, pornography, terrorism, etc.) and addiction apart, the Internet is a remarkable means of communication that can help spread the gospel of reform of education. A plethora of organizations (liberal and conservative, loving and hateful) utilize this communication vehicle to disseminate ideas and recruit members. Educators, too, can take advantage of the World Wide Web to advocate the reform of education in cyberspace in manifold ways. In fact, many already do.

We should be inspired by youngsters like Bill Wetzel from *Power to the Youth* who initiated a Web-based movement by himself. In fact, after forming grassroots support groups at the local level, teachers should create a cyber network of professionals committed to the same cause. Each group--and individuals as well--can create its own Web page with links to all affiliated members of the grassroots movement for reform of education in freedom. We should also use e-mail to communicate our message to every relevant individual, organization and association in cyberspace.

The Internet, in spite of its misuse and abuse, can be a wondrous tool for transforming consciousness. And let's not forget that several groups, some of which are the antithesis of human development, are aggressively propagating their wretched plan of action. Hate and extremist groups, religious fanatics, xenophobic organizations, among other equally vicious tendencies, are vividly present in cyberspace. They are always procuring new members and diffusing their message of fear, divisiveness--and ignorance. They must be counteracted by those who believe that human development (the education of mind, heart and spirit in freedom, justice and love) is the hope for the future. Teachers have the opportunity to be the harbingers of a new era in education and social reform. All we have to do is act; now!

The use of the Internet in organizing and promoting different causes has been evinced in many instances. Activists of all sorts have been successful in recruiting and mobilizing people akin to their objectives. In fact, a Berkeley, California-based activist group that promotes nonviolent direct actions against opposing forces, has recently admitted that the Internet was crucial to organizing the more than forty-five thousand protesters who filled Seattle's streets during the World Trade Organization meeting in December of 1999. This illustrates the extraordinary communication and mobilization power of the Internet; a power that we must use for our reformative cause.

We have the opportunity to put technology to a good use for an honorable cause: the integral development of the human being through education. With creativity, imagination and a network of committed teachers, we can, indeed, make an extraordinary difference in the world. However, we should not delay one single moment, for the opposite forces are already advancing, aggressively, their disheartening concept of humanity as selfish, greedy and voracious consumers fulfilling tedious economic functions. They do not have a vision for the future because they are blinded by ignorance; of themselves and the present circumstances of our times.

Since the World Wide Web is a modern sibling of a globalized economic culture, the movement for the reform of education must be internationalized as well. Although we must first strengthen our position at home, we should gradually connect with colleagues in the international community of teachers, for the ultimate goal is education for human development--everywhere! Moreover, teachers in other parts of the world can share valuable information with like-minded peers in an international reform of education movement. They have different views and experiences, depending on the cultural and political background of their nation. Besides, isn't globalization the wave of the future? So, let's ride it!

How to globalize the reform of education movement?

When Dr. Robert Muller, former Assistant Secretary-General of the United Nations and Chancellor of the UN University for Peace in Costa Rica, developed The World Core Curriculum, he realized it was time children learned from the global point of view. He divided the curriculum into four distinct categories: our planetary home and place in the universe, the family of humanity, our place in time, and the miracle of individual human life. It has been a commendable attempt to internationalize the educational system based on general human needs; and a great step toward the reform of education.

Despite Dr. Muller's efforts, The World Core Curriculum is unbeknownst to many--if not most-- teachers. Perhaps if a coalition of educators committed to the globalization of the reform of education were actively engaged, teachers everywhere would not only be informed but would participate in this and many similar ventures. Incidentally, this is only one of many movements geared toward liberating schooling from the materialism of the world's educational machine. And as the world community becomes more intertwined by globalization, an international system of education, developed by broad-minded teachers and leading educational thinkers, is becoming a necessity of the times. Furthermore, if the ideal of world democracy is to be solidly established, a common approach to human development, a sense of world citizenship modeled on the principles of freedom, justice, unity and right human relations is *sine qua non*. We are talking about a vision of society where the purpose of education is wisdom.

In order to globalize the reform of education movement, it is necessary to create a network of like-minded educators worldwide. There are several ways to set it off. Two that seem likely to engender immediate results are: the appropriate use of the Internet and international exchange programs. The latter should be designed to sharing the vision of a new educational philosophy in which humanity is the ultimate beneficiary. Although there already are some successful international exchange programs (the Fulbright Scholarship Program, for instance), they primarily focus on traditional academic values. However, similar initiatives could be introduced with international reform of education as the main objective in the international exchanging of teachers.

What has the potential to strengthen even more this possibility is the participation of non-educational entities. Involving different organizations, associations and businesses could be of utmost importance to the movement. For example, organizations such as Amnesty International and businesses like Oxfam, whose mission statement is "to work with others to overcome poverty and suffering in the world," could play a fundamental role in supporting the advent of a new era in educational reform worldwide. Educators for human development working together with organizations promoting human rights and businesses concerned with human suffering and poverty; what a powerful partnership that would be!

In fact, from all the several venues that would facilitate the globalization of the reform of education movement, none is more powerful and effective than establishing coalitions of groups, associations and organizations committed to an international reform of education for human development. Such coalitions have proven particularly successful in the environmental movement, whose strategies have gained substantial strength since joining forces with labor unions. Together, they were able to gather tens of thousands of demonstrators on the streets of Seattle, Washington, and completely paralyzed the World Trade Organization meeting. Most importantly, they generated extraordinary international publicity to their cause.

It is about time educator reformers become more actively involved in the struggle for liberation of the human spirit. Like other conscientious citizens, we need to draw attention to the problems of education for economic functions worldwide. Let the international spotlight shine on the stage of the reform of education for integral human development.

How to begin uniting the teaching class, immediately?

Although internationalizing the reform of education movement is important--and inevitable--we must first consolidate the teaching class locally; in every country, state, city and school. However, the entire process really begins to unfold with YOU, the individual teacher. It is your responsibility to get involved and act.

You can unleash the entire operation by committing yourself to supporting your colleagues, students and schools. It is called solidarity; which by the way, was the name of the movement that eventually set Poland free from its oppressive communist government in the late 1980's. By applying the same principle of solidarity you, too, can liberate the whole of education from the shackles of intellectual and economic domination.

However, you will need help; plenty of it, not only from your fellow- teachers but from the society you serve. And the first and most important ally to cajole is parents; they are the ones who make up the bulk of public opinion regarding educational issues. You must educate them just as much as you educate their children, though the subject matter is quite different in nature. In addition, whenever you form or become a member of a grassroots group, make sure to create an alliance--subtle or downright--with parents. It is the most important relationship in the struggle to regain control of educational practices. If you as a teacher succeed in developing a strong solidarity with your colleagues, and, at the same time, receive the support of parents, you automatically become a powerful force in education; one which the bureaucracy cannot withstand.

Ultimately, you can begin uniting the teaching class by truly dedicating yourself to education and all its vital elements, i.e., teachers, students, society--and freedom. Once you commit, you will inevitably take action; and the quality of your actions shall pave the way to a brighter future.

FINAL WORD

The word reform is ubiquitous in many segments of society these days. The public opinion and politicians talk about welfare reform, tax reform, political campaign reform, and, obviously, education reform. The latter, however, distinguishes itself in twofold ways: everyone seems to agree there is a need for it, and it is the only reform that can affect all the others.

Ostensibly, education is the most important question occupying people's mind today. Unfortunately, most do not realize that education is not merely a matter of acquiring academic skills verifiable through standardized test results, but a learning process for individual and social transformation. It is absolutely futile to discuss the problems of escalating violence, insufficient health care, environmental devastation, etc. without taking education as the common denominator in the equation. There should be no doubt in anyone's mind that education is central to all our social problems, and not only an issue regarding the economic prosperity of the individual and society.

Throughout the twentieth century education has been geared toward economic functionalism. Except for a few isolated movements, the educational system has been committed to promoting utilitarian knowledge that benefits scientific, technological and economic expansion. Meanwhile, a multitude of problems have been escalating concomitantly with the achievements of modern civilization. From environmental disasters to the threat of a nuclear holocaust--which remains an ominous possibility--more problems have been added on to the arsenal of self-inflicted misery. Not knowing what to do and unable to halt the wheel of "progress," we have been taking the time hoping that science, technology and economic expansion will solve our problems, though often times they can be some of the main culprits aggravating our predicament. Time, however, is a luxury running out faster than the tropical rain forests in the world. It is time to take action through one of the most effective means: education.

While education in the twentieth century was dedicated to improving scientific, technological and economic development--which allowed humanity to go from wagons to rockets in less than one hundred years-- the same period was marked by extremely violent upheavals. In fact, the bloodiest century of history has been marked by two world wars, numerous revolutions, hideous crimes against humanity, the slaughter of the environment and culminating with the threat of a nuclear holocaust. Thus, even the casual observer of social circumstances today, can notice that the obsessive pursuit of intellectual expansion has led to the demise of emotional and spiritual intelligence. Furthermore, in the process of accumulating intellectual knowledge, humanity has lost, unwittingly, the longing for wisdom. If there is faith in recovering the desire to be wise, education is definitely the best synonym for hope.

Now that we have embarked on a new--and critical--century, there is not an iota of time left to waste. If positive transformation is to take place in the world, it must begin with the education of children, for they are the ones who will have to deal with the accumulated problems first hand. I am convinced, in fact, I do not have a modicum of doubt, that education is the main and perhaps the only vehicle that can transform the individual and usher the world to a new social order. It has been proven that this cannot be achieved otherwise; be it by laws, conventions, organizations or any other initiative that does not begin and end with human development.

The dream of maintaining materialistic expansion while individual human development deteriorates is over. The social consequences generated by excessive greed and selfishness in a cut-throat competitive economic system (e.g., hatred, violence, poverty, individual human misery, etc.), have all been swept under the rug of economic prosperity. On the surface all is wonderful and beautiful; underneath is filthy and repulsive. Thus, the dream of material abundance has become a frightening nightmare of spiritual poverty. Education is the alarm clock that can wake us up to a new day to plan better and lasting dreams.

In the meantime, the bureaucrats of ignorance continue on selling--literally--their educational policies to the public and the educational community. They have a "vision" for the technology-oriented education (economy) of the future. They demand better standardized test results while blaming teachers for the ills of utilitarian education. They spend (our) funds as they deem important to the development of the economic functionalism of education. They enslave the child to a premature and excessive process of acquisition of information, so they can be ready to compete in the dominant global economy manipulated by a coalition of gigantic corporations. They devise an educational system in which the child will grow up in front of a glaring computer monitor screen, aging without the emotional and spiritual development that will make him a full-fledged human being. In the end, the only remaining part that is truly human is the body.

Although the struggle against the bureaucratic forces will be arduous and querulous, we have discussed many possibilities for transformative action. We know we can--and must--unite within the profession in order to bring positive change to education and society. We have a unique opportunity to affect the core of social issues, the power, means and the duty to generate results. Certainly, the reactionary forces will label us as a rebellious professional group or other poignant pejorative term; it is part of the defamation propaganda effort. But with integrity and exemplary commitment to human development, we will prove to society at large that we do not fight against anybody. We fight on behalf of everyone.

The human family has become dysfunctional. It is like a diseased body in need of medical care. Education is the heart of the social organism pumping nutrients to every individual cell of the body. However, because of the unhealthy educational diet of the system, an urgent transplant of this organ has become necessary for survival in the new millennium.

So, I ask you all, teachers of the world: what are you going to do with your calling to teach? Are you going to serve humanity or an economic machinery that has made a slave of you as well? Are you going to help rescuing the human spirit or contribute to its demise? What are you going to do as the most influential professional in society in these times of unprecedented challenges? Are you going to be active or passive? Are you going to divide or unite? The answers to these and many other related questions could be the difference between a promising future and none at all. The choice is yours--and so is the responsibility.

RESOURCES

Association Montessori Internationale of the United
States of America
410 Alexander Street, Rochester, New York, NY 14607-
1028
Phone: (716) 461-5920 Fax: (716) 461-0075
Web site: http://www.montessori-ami.org
AMI/USA promotes the principles of Dr. Maria
Montessori to the education of children. It aims to help
children to attain their full potential in our
multicultural society.

Association of Waldorf Schools in North America
3911 Bannister Road, Fair Oaks, CA 95628
Phone: (916) 961-0927 Fax: (916) 961-0715
Web site: http://www.awsna.org
AWSNA is an organization dedicated to promoting the
education philosophy of Rudolf Steiner, the father of
Waldorf Education. Steiner's insight brought to
education the concept of an intimate relationship
between the physical, the psychological, and the
spiritual in the learning human being. This approach
is solidly based on the principles of Anthroposophy,
which embraces a spiritual view of the human being
and the cosmos in an attempt to comprehend the
nature and essence of human life.

Center for Commercial-Free Public Education
1714 Franklin St., Nos. 100-306, Oakland, CA 94612
Phone: (510) 268-1100 Fax: (510) 268-1277 Toll Free:
(800) 867-5841
Web site: http://www.commercialfree.org
The Center for Commercial-Free Public Education
works to find low-cost community solutions to
problems in education; fights unequal education, in
particular the corporate takeover of public schools and
Channel One.

Educators for Social Responsibility
23 Garden Street, Cambridge, MA 02138
Phone: (617) 492-1764 Fax: (617) 864-5164
Web site: http://www.benjeryi.com/esr
Educators for Social Responsibility's primary mission

is to help young people develop the convictions and skills to shape a safe, sustainable, and just world. Its goal is to make teaching social responsibility a core practice in the schooling and upbringing of children.

Institute of Noetic Sciences
475 Gate Five Road, Suite 300, Sausalito, CA 94965
Phone: (415) 331-5650 Fax: (415) 331-5673
Web site: http://www.noetic.org/ions/about/index.asp
The Institute of Noetic Sciences is a nonprofit organization, research foundation, and educational institution dedicated to exploring our knowledge and understanding of the potential of the human mind, full capacity of the human spirit, and the profound societal transformation occurring today. Its members are drawn together by the shared vision of a future that is more just, humane, sustainable, tolerant and affirming for all.

Lucis Trust.
113 University, 11th Floor, New York, NY 10003, USA
3 Whitehall Court, Suite 54, London, England SWIA 2EF
1 Rue de Varembé (3E), Case Postale 31, 1211 Geneva 20, Switzerland
Web site: http://www.lucistrust.org/
Lucis Trust is a nonpolitical and nonsectarian organization with many activities dedicated to the establishment of right human relations. It promotes the education of the human mind towards recognition and practice of the spiritual principles and values upon which a stable and interdependent world society may be based. Lucis Trust is committed to promoting love of humanity and service of the human race.

National Association for Legal Support of Alternative Schools
P.O. Box 2823, Santa Fé, NM 87504
Phone: (505) 471-6928
NALSAS is an organization that helps individuals and organizations locate, evaluate, and create viable alternatives to traditional schooling approaches.

National Coalition of Alternative and Community Schools
1266 Rosewood Unit 1, Ann Arbor, MI 48104-6205
Phone: (734) 668-9171

86

Web site: http://www.ncacs.org
NCACS is a non-profit coalition of schools, groups and
individuals committed to creating an egalitarian society
by actively working against racism, ageism, and all forms
of social, political, and economic oppression. The
coalition's objectives and purposes are to support an
educational process that empowers people to actively
and collectively direct their lives; restore the active
control of education to students, parents, teachers, and
community members who are mostly directly affected;
and developing tools and skills to work for social justice.

National Coalition of Education Activists
P.O. Box 679, Rhinebeck, New York, NY12572
Phone: (914) 876-4580 Fax: (914) 876-4461
E-mail: rfbs@aol.com
NCEA is a multiracial network of families, school staff,
union and community activists, and others organizing
for equity and fundamental changes in local school
districts. Its purpose is to support activists in their
efforts to develop, promote, and implement progressive
school reforms, to provide a counter to the right, and to
fight racism and other forms of institutional bias.

Partners in Human Rights Education
University of Minnesota Human Rights Center/MN
Advocates for Human Rights
229-19th Ave. South, Room 439, Minneapolis, MN 55455
Phone: (612) 626-0041 Fax: (612) 625-2011
Web site:
http://www1.umn.edu/humanrts/peace/peaceedu/bin
der1.html
Partners in Human Rights Education is a program
designed to introduce international human rights and
responsibilities to students of all ages. The Partners
Program uses the framework of the Universal Declaration
of Human Rights and the Convention of the Rights of the
Child to help students to understand and appreciate
common human values.

Society for Educational Reconstruction
c/o Dr. Darrol Bussler, Mankato State University,
Mankato, MN 56002-8400
Phone: (507) 389-6222/(612) 455-8466 Fax: (507) 389-
5854

E-mail: darrol.bussler@mankato.msus.edu
The primary mission of the Society for Educational
Reconstruction is to further the understanding and
practice of educational reconstruction philosophy. The
organization draws educators and social service
professionals dedicated to personal, social, and political
transformation through education. Its goals include:
social democracy; cooperative power exercised toward
moral ends; global order; and the possibility of self-
transformation for each individual. It also serves as a
support network for educators who function as social
change activists.

Teaching Tolerance: The Southern Poverty Law Center
400 Washington Avenue, Montgomery, AL 36104
Web site:
http://www.splcenter.org/teachingtolerance/tt-
index.html
Teaching Tolerance was founded in 1991 to provide
teachers with resources and ideas to help promote
harmony in the classroom--and society. It is an
educational program of The Southern Poverty Law
Center, a nonprofit legal and education foundation.

The Robert Muller School International Coordinating
Center
6005 Royaloak Drive, Arlington, TX 76016, USA
Phone: 1(817) 654-1018 Fax: 1(817) 654-1028
Web site: http://www.unol.org/rms/
The center provides information on The World Core
Curriculum and the Robert Muller Schools, which is
based on a fourfold curriculum: our planetary home and
place in the universe, the family of humanity, our place
in time, and the miracle of the individual human life.

Triangles in Education
Office of the Caduceator
56 Falkland, Skelmersdale, Lancs., WN8 6RA, United
Kingdom
Phone/Fax: (+44) 01695 556664
Web site:
http://freespace.virgin.net/caduceator.clh/TrinEd.html
Triangles in Education is an international, spiritually
motivated mental networking of educators, supportive of
all efforts to promote the strengthening of the light, love-

wisdom and power of the Soul in education. It believes that there is great hope for the widespread emergence of educational systems which can meet the spiritual needs of the earth's six billion strong population, and so help to dissolve the threat which an unspiritualized humanity poses to the rest of Nature.

ABOUT THE AUTHOR

Sebastian de Assis is an inspiring writer and educator with more than 23 years of experience in education. His eclectic professional background ranges from teaching in both traditional and alternative settings, from first grade through college level in Europe, Latin America and the United States. He has traveled extensively through numerous countries in four continents, which has bestowed upon him extraordinary empirical knowledge of multiculturalism and the international community. He is fluent in Spanish, Portuguese and French.

His writings and presentations reveal threefold concerns: to foster integral human development, enhance the quality of education according to human needs--instead of economic demands--and to promote the prosperity of the group in the developmental process of the individual. He is available for presentations, consultations and professional development training. He may be reached at The Educational Center Press, P.O. Box 443, Corvallis, OR 97339-0443, or at edupress@peak.org.

BOOK REVIEW

Here is your chance to review this book. Let us know what you liked about it--and what you didn't--and send your comments to The Educational Center Press, P.O. Box 443, Corvallis, OR 97339-0443, or at edupress@peak.org . The author welcomes your feedback. We will incorporate your suggestions and opinions into future editions and promotional literature. Thank you for participating in this readership review process.

ORDER FORM

Yes, I would like to order _____ copies of Teachers of the World, Unite! at $10.95 each, plus $3 for postage and handling per order of 3 books or less (4 books or more postage and handling charges are waived). Enclosed is a check or money order in the amount of $_____ payable to The Educational Center Press. Send your order to The Educational Center Press, P.O. Box 443, Corvallis, OR 97339-0443. Inquire about special discount for quantity order.

In order to expedite your order, please print form clearly.

Name: _____

Address: _____

City, State, Zip _____

Phone (   ) _____ Fax (   ) _____

e-mail _____

Please photocopy and remit.